1000 ideas for term papers in WORLD LITERATURE

ROBERT A. FARMER

WARNER MEMORIAL LIBRARY
EASTERN UNIVERSITY
ST. DAVIDS, PA 19087-3696

ARC BOOKS, INC. New York

PN 61 .F3
Farmer, Robert Allen.
1000 ideas for term papers
in world literature

Published by ARC BOOKS, INC.
219 Park Avenue South, New York, N. Y. 10003
Copyright © Robert Farmer, 1970
All Rights Reserved
*No part of this book may be reproduced, by any means,
without permission in writing from the publisher, except
by a reviewer who wishes to quote brief excerpts in
connection with a review in a magazine or newspaper.*
Library of Congress Catalog Card Number 71-80882
Printed in the United States of America

Preface

THIS book is designed to assist the student in writing a relevant, successful paper in World Literature. It is meant to be a practical and stimulating guide—it will not, however, replace the effort necessary for an understanding of the work.

I have gathered what I hope is a representative selection of topics to demonstrate the wealth of approaches that a student can make to the subject matter. Many of the topics suggest comparisons of themes, ideas, or styles, so that the more involved student will get a broader view of World Literature.

Contents

Preface	5

I. A Short Guide to the Art of Term-Paper Writing

1. Introduction	9
2. Selecting a Topic	11
3. Research Sources	16
4. Organization and Development	18
5. Fundamentals of Form	21
6. Term Paper Tips	26

II. Term Paper Topics

A Note on the Use of This Section	29
Term Paper Topics	31
CLASSIC	31
MIDDLE AGES	39
RENAISSANCE	42
FRENCH NEO-CLASSIC	52
ENGLISH NEO-CLASSIC	58
FRENCH ROMANTIC	63
GERMAN ROMANTIC	67
ENGLISH ROMANTIC	72
FRENCH REALISM	78
SCANDINAVIAN REALISM	83
POST-ROMANTIC GERMANY	86
VICTORIAN ENGLAND	88
RUSSIA—*19th Century*	93
FRANCE—*19th Century*	98
AMERICA—*Colonial Period to 20th Century*	100
ENGLAND—*20th Century*	113
EUROPE—*20th Century*	119
20TH CENTURY DRAMA	125
AMERICA—*20th Century*	131

Part I

A Short Guide to the Art of Term-Paper Writing

CHAPTER 1

Introduction

Writing an English term paper can be one of the most enjoyable as well as interesting assignments a student can undertake. It can, however, be a most difficult one, too.

A good term paper has a point to make; it should state it clearly and concisely. It always displays sound organization and the effective use of language. Ideally, a term paper teaches something to the writer as well as to the reader.

The first section of this book briefly discusses the necessary elements of a sound paper, from concept to completion. It should help you to develop an efficient and logical method of working with your ideas and to start you thinking creatively about your project.

The second section offers an extensive list of term paper topics to which you can apply these ideas. They should help you to formulate an interesting topic for your particular assignment.

Work is the primary requisite for a good term paper. If you are not interested in World Literature, and you know before you begin to do research for the paper that you are not going to devote much time to this assignment, choose a topic of modest scope and do it competently. On the other hand, if you want to involve yourself completely with the writing of your term paper, try to make a realistic evaluation of your goals and what it will take to reach them.

The intention of this book is to help you choose a topic for a term paper, and to give you suggestions on how to approach the task of writing it. It does not, however, write the paper for you.

CHAPTER 2

Selecting a Topic

SELECTING a topic is the key step in the process of composing a research paper. The topic you select will affect the time needed to research and write the paper as well as the quality of the finished product.

Each student is aware of his or her needs in writing a research paper. The topic should be chosen accordingly. For this reason, each topic suggested is accompanied by a Roman numeral to indicate the degree of difficulty.

Topics marked (I) are considered to be the most simple, and those marked (III) the most sophisticated; however, these ratings should not discourage you from using any topic that suits you.

The first step in selecting a topic lies in choosing the material that your paper will discuss. This may be an author or a particular work in a literary movement. On the other hand, you may decide to let the subject be determined by the approach you select. There are at least six ways of approaching any subject: biographical, historical, textual, stylistic, thematic and comparative.

Suppose that you have been assigned William Faulkner's *The Sound and the Fury*. Here are some of the directions that each of the six approaches might suggest:

(1) Biographical

Scope: The role of the book in Faulkner's development as a writer.

Approach: Compare with earlier and later works for differences in style and attitude. Is this book in any way a culmination or a beginning of a trend?

(2) Historical

Scope: The effect of southern life on the book.

Approach: Could the same story have been set in another region?

(3) Textual

Scope: Examination of narrative structure.

Approach: Is there an order to the revelation of events and of the characters' point of view? What is its over-all effect?

(4) Stylistic

Scope: What is the source of the book's impact?

Approach: Rewrite several paragraphs in your own words. How does Faulkner's use of the language differ from yours? How is his more powerful?

(5) Thematic

Scope: Someone has said, "Every story boils down to one paragraph." Is this true of The Sound and the Fury? *If so, does it fit into one of the main themes which run through Faulkner's work?*

(6) Comparative

Scope: Faulkner states, "Dilsey is one of my own favorite characters, because she is brave, courageous, gentle, and honest." How does she differ from other characters whom Faulkner created?

Another consideration is to determine the *breadth and the depth* of your topic. Make sure the information you have collected in researching your topic is sufficient to cover your entire subject. In addition, careful consideration of your involvement with the subject in terms of interest and time will avoid the use of superficial and irrelevant details.

Finally, evaluate the topic in its relationship to the course for which it was assigned.

Choose your topic to complement your skills as a writer and thinker. More important, do not choose one that will overemphasize your intellectual weaknesses. If you have a rather prosaic mind, avoid poetic analysis, since you may not be capable of appreciating the subtleties of imagery and tone that distinguish the poet's work. Similarly, don't be entrapped by whimsical or "gimmicky" topics, unless you have the flair to handle them successfully. If inspiration seems to fail you, your wisest course will be to aim for a modest topic that you can handle competently.

Such a topic is one on which you can use organization, thoroughness, and careful style as a substitute for real creativity. Such a topic usually involves strict comparison or close analysis of a narrowly defined topic. With only a small area of material to be covered, it can—and must—be treated well. A short but crucial scene of a play may reveal much about the structure and theme of the play as a whole and serve as an important link in the actions that lead to the climax.

This type of topic will also sharpen your perception and widen your understanding of the entire work. A single speech or passage or description from a novel may display character development or the author's point of view or may be a good example of the author's literary style. In any case, such a topic should have the potential for examples, which can be used to fortify your points and lend weight to your arguments.

Your topics should have certain limits, imposed partly by you and partly by the nature of the subject matter. Your definition of the topic will affect the entire procedure of research, organization and composition. The problem of definition can best be understood by examining the effect that a too-narrow or too-broad topic can have upon a paper.

Most students either overestimate their capabilities or underestimate the subject. A realistic attitude toward the length and quality of the paper that you wish to produce will spare you a great deal of dismay the day before it is due. Don't hesitate to consider your interest in the course and the amount of time you are willing to spend doing research as factors in the type you choose. If your ambitions are limited, don't involve yourself in discussions of obscure symbolism or in devising theories about an author's purpose. You will undoubtedly be exhausted before your subject is, and, what is worse, you will wind up with bits of unrelated information which are difficult to rework or to put together into an intelligible whole.

When choosing a topic or developing an approach to a subject, keep in view the nature of the course for which the paper was assigned. Try to think of your paper as a learning process rather than as a collection of facts. You should also attempt to discern the motives that lie behind the assignment; in other words, determine what skills or points of view your teacher wants you to acquire in writing the paper. It may have been intended primarily as an exercise in organization and logical presentation, in which case a relatively simple and straightforward topic will be most suitable. A paper may also be assigned to introduce breadth or depth into a sketchy survey course. In this instance, your wisest choice of subject will be an author or a literary period that has been omitted from the syllabus because of limited time, or one that was discussed only briefly. An alternative would be to choose a common theme or image and treat it in such a manner as to unify the various elements of the course.

CHAPTER 3

Research Sources

Two kinds of source material are available to you: primary and secondary. You may want to use only primary sources, such as an author's works, but if you have only a hazy idea of your subject, secondary sources—works of criticism—can be invaluable. Not only will they throw light on your subject, but they will present varying points of view, which you can support or contradict. Where do you find this secondary source material? First, try the card-catolog index under the author's name, then try the following:

Encyclopedias

Special literary encyclopedias, such as *Cassell's Encyclopedia of Literature* and the *Oxford Classical Dictionary*, can serve as an introduction to the author and his tradition. You will find details of authors, titles, characters, themes, and terminology used in *The Reader's Companion to World Literature*, as well as in *The Oxford Companion* series to American, English, French, and classical literature.

Bibliographies

Bibliographies serve the same purpose as does the card-catalog subject index; in addition, they often indicate the basic or best books on your subject. Each field has its own bibliography; you can find yours in a bibliography of bibliographies, such as the *Bibliographic Index.*

Periodical Indices

Periodical indices are catalogs of articles published in magazines. Indices that you may find useful include: *The Reader's Guide to Periodical Literature; Poole's Index to Periodical Literature* (1802-1906); and the *Publication of the Modern Language Association* (PMLA) *Journal,* which has recent biographical as well as periodical information.

Footnotes

The footnotes in a comprehensive study of your author's works or his period may yield numerous leads to useful books.

To verify the reliability of your sources, it would be advisable to answer the following questions:

1. When was the work written? Have there been important developments in your field since its copyright date?
2. What are the author's qualifications?
3. Does the source approach your subject directly or indirectly?
4. Is the author biased? Does the author bear some personal grudge against your subject? Does his attitude show? Is his criticism of the work justifiable?
5. Is your source well footnoted? Critical works without footnotes are often honest and valid, but they may prove very difficult for you to use as reference sources.

CHAPTER 4

Organization and Development

WHEN you have completed the search for the information that you will need to construct your paper, it is time to think about developing a system to gather those facts and opinions which are pertinent to your hypothesis. The random pieces must be fitted together to form a logical and satisfying pattern. Perhaps the following biographical notes will be of help to you:

Biographical Notes

As you find books and articles that are relevant to your topic, make a 3"×5" note-card for each one, listing:

1. Author
2. Title
3. Publication data
4. Call number
5. Page numbers of sections that you want to use.

This may seem a nuisance to you while doing it, but it will be very helpful in putting together your rough draft.

Organizational Notes

When you are confident that you have sufficient

materials for your paper, your next step is the organization of your paper.

Writing a research paper requires technique. Before trying to systematize, read your notes carefully several times. This will accustom you fully with your main topic.

After reviewing your information, separate your notes into two or three categories, corresponding to the highpoints of your paper. Organize each category by treating it as an entity.

1. Introduction
2. Developmental
3. Conclusion

By doing this you can determine where (if any) weak spots exist and make corrections.

Your next step should be to develop a detailed outline. The structuring of information is a necessary step in writing your term paper. An outline will keep all your thoughts and ideas in correct, understandable order, making the actual writing of the paper much easier for you.

The First Draft

In writing the first draft, *logic and clarity* should be your main guidelines. Without them, your paper will be a mass of senseless phrases.

Do not try to edit anything while writing the first draft. First, get all your ideas down and then go back and edit your work.

Before writing the final draft, read your first draft through carefully and objectively. Find its faults and correct them. Always remember logic and clarity; without them your paper will be worthless.

The methodical work of recognizing the limits of your topic, knowing your facts, and adhering to a fairly formal plan for presenting information and argument is done to facilitate the actual writing process. All of the steps mentioned so far can be done in short stretches of time, at irregular intervals, thus minimizing the tedium that is involved in the preparation of a long term paper. A paper that has been well planned in the manner described should require only one draft before typing, and can be composed at the rate of about two to four pages an hour. While writing it, constantly remind yourself that a paper must have a hypothesis. Concentrate on using your facts to state it, develop it, and prove its validity. In addition, the preliminary work you have done should enable you to inject flair into your writing and encourage an imaginative presentation.

CHAPTER 5

Fundamentals of Form

FORM is not necessarily a rigid pattern in the writing of a term paper, but rather an inherent quality in all good writing. It is a sort of direction which guides the reader. Form is the structural manifestation of logic.

When you develop the form of your paper, let it be as creative as your thoughts. Bear in mind the kind of information you are trying to present and then decide how it can best be put in order. Some topics require a great deal of introductory material in order to acquaint the reader with the background necessary for a full understanding of the topic. Others may demand numerous examples to prove your thesis. The variations are endless, but all involve some sort of recognizable pattern which serves as guide to both the author and the reader. The simplest categorical divisions include:

1. Statement of Purpose
2. Development
3. Conclusion

The statement of purpose may be modified to include a brief introduction to the various themes that you will be developing. The development may perhaps include several subtopics, marked by formal or implied chapter divisions, each of which has its own purpose and conclusion in relation to the overall topic. The conclusion can be rendered more effective by summarizing the arguments presented in the development to give your "conclusion" an air of inevitability. In any case, the form you use should reflect the organization of your outline, and succeed in giving your paper a feeling of progression.

Making up footnotes and a bibliography is probably the most tedious aspect of composing a term paper. The most annoying problem you will encounter when footnoting is determining when you should or should not cite a reference. Statistics, unusual or controversial dates (such as that of Shakespeare's birth), and quotations should always be footnoted. Opinions, critical analysis by another, or interpretations should also be cited. You can avoid using a formal footnote, if you have already cited the work, by mentioning the work of the author in the body of the text, especially if the reference is well known or is one that you have used frequently in the course. If you are dealing with only one work, textual references can be cited by merely including the page number in parentheses after the statement.

When in doubt about whether to footnote or not, remember it is always better to include them. Footnotes are a sort of insurance against the suspicions of plagiarism.

Footnotes may be presented in several ways, depending on the requirements of your instructor. Some insist that the citations appear at the bottom of each page, whereas others may permit you to list them in a separate section at the end of your paper. The latter is much easier for you, but harder for the reader. Several variations for presenting footnotes exist, but style is far less important than consistency. The author's full name, book title, place of publication, publisher, date of publication, and the pages to which you are referring should appear in standard footnote form. The first line of the citation should be indented, and each footnote should be separated from the others by two spaces. Notes themselves should be single spaced.

Mark Twain, *The Adventures of Huckleberry Finn* (New York: Washington Square Press, 1960), p. 57.

Notice in the example that the author's surname follows his Christian name (the opposite of the form for bibliographic citation). A comma divides the author's name from his work, and a period closes the footnote. Punctuation is not used between the title of the book and the parentheses containing the publication data. Other procedures include: underlining the book title, inserting a colon between the place of publication and the publisher's name, and putting a comma at the end of the parentheses. The form for periodicals resembles that for regular works, with a few exceptions. Usually the publisher and place of publication are not included, but the volume and issue numbers, separated by a comma, take their place after the titles. Most newspaper and magazine articles do not list an author, but if they do, it should precede the title of the article and name of the publication. Examples of the most common types of form are shown as follows:

The Atlantic Monthly, Vol. X, 123 (1948), p. 65

D. H. Lawrence, "Symbolism in Nature." *The Modern Poet*, Vol. III, 16 (Jan. 18, 1931), p. 23.

New York Times, July 12, 1911, p. 49.

For a work that is being cited more than once

in your paper, there are two shortcuts that you may employ after you have formally listed the necessary information the first time it is used. The author's last name, followed by a comma and the page number, is an easy method of reference, although if you are using more than one work by him be sure to include a shorthand method of differentiating the various books.

Example:

>Hawthorne, p. 89.

or

>Hawthorne, *Scarlet Letter*, p. 67.

If the footnote, immediately preceding, cites the same author and work as the one to which you are referring, use the abbreviation *Ibid.*, (always underlined) and give the page number. This will be sufficient.

Example:

>Emerson, p. 78.
>*Ibid.*, p. 65

The bibliography is an important clue to the amount of work and thought that have gone into the creation of your term paper. A long bibliography should be divided into the categories of:

1. Sources
2. Supplementary Works
3. Periodicals and Newspapers

The form for a bibliography entry differs from footnote form in only two ways (with the exception of the page number), each containing the same information. 1) A bibliography entry lists the author's surname first; entries are arranged within categories in alphabetical order. 2) Parentheses are omitted from around the publication data.

> Dickens, Charles. *Bleak House*. New York: The New American Library of World Literature, Inc., 1964.

In the above example, note that the author's name and the title are followed by periods. The date and the publisher are separated by a comma.

CHAPTER 6

Term Paper Tips

THE following might assist you in the writing of your term paper:

1. Type your paper if possible. This always creates a favorable impression.

2. Corrections suggest mistakes. If you have to cross out a word, or insert one, consider retyping that page.

3. Be sure to proofread your paper before handing it in for grading. Small errors will annoy the reader and dull the impact of your ideas. They will also lower your grade!

4. If you have gathered many quotes in the research of this paper, use some of them. Do not, however, include all of them in the body of your paper, unless they enhance the finished copy.

5. Your ideas support only a certain number of words. Repetition may weaken your point and suggest an insufficient amount of information gathered and research done on your part.

6. Never assume that your reader will be familiar with your subject. You must prove each step of your hypothesis.

7. Make sure that your title is an interesting one. The title of a paper should serve the dual purposes of defining your paper's scope to some degree and catching the reader's interest at the very beginning of the paper.

8. In papers over five or ten pages long, some

division of the text into chapters can be useful. This division not only highlights your ideas and aids the reader in his comprehension, but also forces you to make your points with greater care. Formal chapter breaks are not necessary; a line of asterisks is sufficient.

Part II

Term Paper Topics

A Note on the Use of This Section

In the pages that follow, you will find a selection of topics for term papers in the field of World Literature. The examples range over the whole of the World Literature field. They are drawn from novels, poetry, and plays.

The topics have been assembled to inspire as well as inform you. They will give you a good indication of the many directions that a successful paper can take when one instills a bit of imagination and flair into his writing.

Each subject is viewed from a different literary angle. In choosing a topic this should be kept in mind. Make sure you select the approach that you can handle competently.

There are more than a thousand topics on these pages, since the subject matter, the points of view, and the germinal ideas that constitute them can be recombined in many ways. If you see a good approach to one of Shakespeare's plays, you can use the same approach on one of Shaw's or O'Neill's plays.

Topics marked (I) are considered to be the most simple, and those marked (III) the most sophisticated; however, these arbitrary ratings should not discourage you from using any topic that suits you.

The sample topic shown below illustrates the typographic arrangement used throughout. Note that the first paragraph indicates the author and the source. The second paragraph gives you the suggested title of your paper. The third paragraph outlines the scope of your paper, and the fourth paragraph contains a suggested approach for you to follow in writing it.

SAMPLE TOPIC

Goethe: *Faust*
Dante: *The Divine Comedy*

TITLE: *Faust* and *The Divine Comedy*

SCOPE: *Compare and contrast these two works in terms of style and structure.*

APPROACH: Can *Faust* be called an allegory? Why? Is *Faust* an epic? Are the structures tight and objective in both? (III)

Term Paper Topics

Classic

Homer: *Iliad*
Odyssey

THE CONFLICT BETWEEN HUMANS AND SUB-HUMANS IN HOMER

Trace the development of the various subhuman creatures in Homer.

Discuss Homer's use of the subhuman or animal adversary in the *Iliad* (the Chimera) and in the *Odyssey* (Cyclops). (II)

Homer: *Odyssey*

THE LOSS OF HOME IN THE ODYSSEY

What is the effect of the loss of home to the characters in the story?

What is the significance of home land? What does it mean in metaphysical terms? (I)

Dante: *The Divine Comedy*
Homer: *Iliad*
Odyssey

THE *Iliad* AS INFERNO, THE *Odyssey* AS PARADISE

Show the relationship of INFERNO *to the Purgatorio and then relate the* ILIAD *to the* ODYSSEY *in the same way.*

How is the spirit of the *Odyssey* freer from the atmosphere of war and sin of the *Iliad*? (III)

Horace: *Odes*, Book III

HORACE AND THE AUGUSTAN IDEAL

Examine the six "Roman" odes which begin Book III in terms of the Roman ideal of living.

Do they advocate the traditional virtues of moderation, hardiness, etc.? What is their significance to Horace? Was he merely flattering Augustus? (II)

Homer: *Iliad*

ACHILLES AS A HERO

Analyze the heroic role of Achilles in the epic.

What are his ideals? What kind of physical stature does he have? How does the author regard his deeds? (III)

Aeschylus: *The Frogs of Aristophanes*

AESCHYLUS AS CRITIC

Examine the critical thought of the time.

Explore the Aristophanic humor in Aeschylus and analyze this comedy of literary criticism. (III)

Aeschylus: *The Oresteia*

THE MORAL USE OF VIOLENCE IN *The Oresteia*

Analyze the use of violence toward a moral end.

Consider all types of violence. How do they arrive at a moral resolution in these plays? (II)

Aeschylus: *The Oresteia*

TRAGEDY AS THE LEGACY OF EVIL IN *The Oresteia*

Analyze the tragic implications of a legacy of evil in the play.

How does evil action in the past affect actions in the present? Why can there be no escape? How is the legacy of evil tragic? (III)

Aeschylus: *The Oresteia*

DISINTEGRATION AND RESTORATION OF ORDER IN *The Oresteia*

Describe how order is destroyed and restored in The Oresteia.

What are the causes of each? Describe the precise nature of the movement from one to the other. (II)

Aeschylus: *The Oresteia*

THE ROLE OF YOUTH IN *The Oresteia*

What is the significance of youth?

What does it represent? How does it affect the dramatic action? (I)

The Plays of Sophocles

THE LOSS OF TRILOGY IN SOPHOCLES

Analyze the tautness of structure in the plays.

Examine the trilogy as a structural form used in Aeschylus. What was its function? What was Sophocles' aim in moving away from the trilogy? (III)

The Works of Sophocles

THE FATE OF THE INDIVIDUAL AS A CENTRAL THEME IN SOPHOCLES

What is the significance of the fate of an individual?

What does the individual represent to Sophocles? Could he have shown this as a trilogy? How does this affect tragedy? (II)

Sophocles: *Ajax*

SOPHOCLES' ATHENE

Examine the two aspects of Athene in AJAX.

(1) She appears as the Homeric duty, dispensing favor on those she loves.
(2) She appears as a grave moral advisor.

What is the significance of this duality? (II)

Sophocles: *Ajax*
          Antigone
          Oedipus Tyrannus

INTENSIFICATION OF TRAGEDY IN SOPHOCLES

Examine the ode of relief and jubilation in AJAX; *the ode before catastrophe in* ANTIGONE *and* OEDIPUS TYRANNUS.

What is the importance of the chorus? Does it underline the fallibility of human reasoning? How does this intensify the tragedy? (II)

Sophocles: *Antigone*

Antigone AS PROPAGANDA

Can the state lay claim to ultimate validity and authority?

Is Creon a spokesman of the state? Or merely driven by an arrogance which only recognizes itself? Does the state have to obey laws which have their origin elsewhere and which remain always beyond reach? (I)

Euripides: *Alcestis*

THE EFFECT OF WOMEN IN *Alcestis*

What is the effect of women in the play?

How do women affect the dramatic action in the play?

Do women act as people or symbols? (I)

Euripides: *Hippolytus*

THE JEALOUSY OF THESEUS

Analyze the jealousy in this character.

Why does he become jealous? How does his jealousy relate to the theme of the play? How does it affect the dramatic action? (II)

Euripides: *Hippolytus*

FATE IN *Hippolytus*

Examine the treatment of fate in this play.

What is the precise meaning of fate in this play? What does fate have to do with the dramatic action? Does the human element win out over the impersonal progress of events? (II)

Euripides: *The Bacchae*

EURIPIDES' ATTITUDE TOWARD MYTH

Study Euripides' opinion on the question of the supremacy of man over the gods. (III)

Vergil: *Aeneid*

THE UNDERWORLD: *Vergil*

Analyze the vision of the afterlife and its landscape.

How does the underworld reflect the characters of those that inhabit it? (I)

Vergil: *Aeneid*
Homer: *Odyssey*

DIDO AND PENELOPE

Compare these two women and their roles.

What significance does each woman have on the overall theme of the epic? Compare Homer's attitude to Vergil's. (II)

Vergil: *Aeneid*

THE HERO AND FREEDOM

Determine the relationship between heroic action and freedom in the AENEID.

Is freedom consonant with heroism in this work? Or is freedom a state of being which the hero rejects? (III)

Vergil: *Aeneid*

FATE IN THE *Aeneid*

Analyze the meaning of fate in the AENEID.

What is the precise meaning of fate? What effect does it have on the characters? Does it add to their stature or detract from it? (I, II)

The Works of Horace

HORACE: THE WHOLE SELF

Trace the ideas of a living man acting upon ideal impulses, practical inducements, animal appetites and yet quite in earnest all the time in his desire to cultivate his mind and improve his character.
(II)

The Works of Horace

CANIDIA THE SORCERESS

Examine the element of mysticism in Horace.

What was Horace's quarrel with Canidia? Did he trust her abilities? What was the significance of the supernatural for Horace? (I, II)

The Works of Horace

WINE AND FIRE: THE METAPHORS OF HORACE

What do "wine" and "fire" represent for Horace?

What was the significance of "wine" for Horace? Was it his love of the past and the communication with nature? Or was he dissatisfied with his own inspiration? What is the significance of "fire?"
(II)

Horace: *Satires*

THE FOUNDATION OF THE *Satires*: HORACE

Show the influence of Lucilius on Horace.

Trace the two Lucilian interests in the satires. We still find personal and social criticism combined with literary criticism, but neither reappears without change. Show how Horace deprecates publicity. (III)

Beowulf

THE ROLE OF THE SUBHUMAN IN *Beowulf*

What is the significance of the subhuman creatures in Beowulf?

Analyze the figures of Grendel and the firedrake. What do they represent? Merely adversaries for the adventure's tribal warriors? Or do they represent something outside the world of men which hates it? (I, II)

Beowulf
Homer: *Iliad*
Odyssey

THE EPIC: *Beowulf* AND HOMER

Contrast the epic form and style in Beowulf *and* Homer.

Compare and contrast the heroic adventure, historical, and geographical background in both. Does each embody profound moral truth? (III)

The Song of Roland
El Cid

ROLAND OR EL CID?

Compare and contrast the two characters in terms of the epic poem.

Are both heroic characters? Are they involved in singular adventures or a variety of adventures?
(II)

Middle Ages

Villon: *The Grand Testament*

DEATH IN THE WORKS OF VILLON

Analyze the theme of death as seen in The Grand Testament.

Discuss the attitude taken by Villon toward this theme and the technique used. What effect do they produce on you? (II)

Villon: *Ballad of Things Known and Unknown*

"I KNOW ALL SAVE MYSELF ALONE"

Examine the role of the "self" in the work of Villon.

What is the "self?" What did it mean to Villon? How does he portray the "self" in the ballad?
(III)

Dante: *The Divine Comedy*

DANTE'S SYMPATHY

How does Dante's humanism appear in THE DIVINE COMEDY?

Evaluate the meaning of Dante's human sympathy in the context of a theological framework which he disputes. (II, III)

Dante: *The Divine Comedy*

EARTHLY PARADISE: *Divine Comedy*

Analyze the nature and treatment of earthly paradise in Dante.

Is earthly paradise possible in the eyes of Dante? If so, to what extent? Show how he indicates false concepts of earthly paradise. (I, II)

Dante: *The Inferno*

THE CIRCLES OF HELL

Literary symbolism and allusion in The Inferno.

Select one or two of the symbols used in this work. Examine these symbols in terms of their significance to the work. Why, in your opinion, were they selected by the author? Are they adequate or would you consider some other symbolization to have been more effective? (III)

Dante: *The Inferno*

THE UNDERWORLD: DANTE

Examine the poet's vision of the afterlife and its landscape.

How does the underworld reflect the characters of those who inhabit it? (II, III)

Dante: *The Inferno*
Vergil: *Aeneid*

THE UNDERWORLD: DANTE AND VERGIL

Compare and contrast the visions of the afterlife by these poets.

What is the significance of the afterlife for each? Does it reflect the characters of its inhabitants?

(III)

Dante: *The Divine Comedy*

THE BEAUTY OF WOMEN IN DANTE

Examine the treatment and attitude toward feminine beauty in THE DIVINE COMEDY.

What is the meaning of beauty? How is it manifested? Is it always good? (I)

Dante: *La Vita Nuova*

BEATRICE: WOMAN OR IMAGE

Analyze the role of Beatrice in the works of Dante.

What does Beatrice represent for Dante? Does she symbolize beatitude and, if so, what is the significance of this beatitude? (II, III)

Snorri Sturlson: *Prose Edda*
Volsung Saga

THE SOURCES OF DAS NIEBELUNGENLIED

Analysis of the development of Niebelungenlied.

Familiarize yourself with the various works which led up to the Niebelungenlied, tracing various heroic, historical and geographical developments.

(III)

Geoffrey Chaucer: "The Nun's Priest's Tale"

THE USE OF SATIRE IN "THE NUN'S PRIEST'S TALE"

"The Nun's Priest's Tale" employs many types of satire on literary conventions, especially the conventions of the heroic narrative. Show how the satirical effects are achieved throughout the Tale.

Examine the language closely with the conventions of the classical epic in mind. Point out the contrasts achieved by Chaucer, especially those between style and subject matter. (II)

Geoffrey Chaucer: "The Pardoner's Tale"

CHAUCER'S COMMENT ON CHANGING SOCIAL STRUCTURES

Explore Chaucer's opinion of the social changes that he observed taking place around him.

Consider the poet's views on the growing strength of the Church and the gradual disintegration of the feudal system. In what ways does the poet reveal his opinions to the reader?

Renaissance

Petrarch: *Songs*
Dante: *La Vita Nuova*

CANZONIERE VS. *La Vita Nuova*

Compare and contrast the poetic styles of Dante and Petrarch.

Analyze the poetic forms in each; do the poems speak for themselves? What is the "sonnet-sequence?" How is it used? (II)

Petrarch: *Sonnets*
Songs

LOVE AND THE PETRARCHAN IMAGINATION

Examine the meaning of Love in the work of Petrarch

Was Petrarch sincere in his love poems? What does Love represent? What does the loved one represent? Who is his "sweetest foe?" How does his attitude affect his handling of 'Love' in the poems? (III)

Petrarch: *Songs*
Selected Works from Provencal

PETRARCH AND PROVENCAL

Compare and contrast the Petrarchan style with the ballads of Provencal.

Analyze the language of love in both; how much of Petrarch is original? Compare the styles of expression in both; which is more sincere? (II, III)

Boccaccio: *The Decameron*
Pillow Book of Sei Shonagon

THE 'CITY'

A cross-cultural investigation of the literary effect of the city.

Almost all major cultures have had their urban centers. However, attitudes toward these centers have differed markedly through the ages. Compare and contrast the attitude in the above works.
(III)

Boccaccio: *The Decameron*

NATURAL AND SOCIAL MAN IN BOCCACCIO

Analyze the treatment of these two aspects of man.

How does the author resolve the conflict between man's natural needs and rights and his social obligations? Which aspect does he value more?

(II)

Boccaccio: *The Decameron*

PLEASURE IN BOCCACCIO

Exame the treatment of 'pleasure' in The Decameron.

What constitutes pleasure? What is its moral quality? Why is it important to Boccaccio? (I)

The Bible: The Flood
Boccaccio: *The Decameron*
Anonymous: *Everyman*

CATASTROPHE

An examination of the characteristics of the literature of catastrophe.

Natural catastrophe produces some of the most intense experiences in the human condition. Artists have transformed these experiences into great art. What are some of the common factors in their technique? What are the differences? What is the significance of each? (II, III)

Boccaccio: *The Decameron*

TRUANCY IN BOCCACCIO

Examine the treatment of social truancy, i.e., the escape from responsibility, in The Decameron.

Why was escape from the normal world necessary? What discoveries and achievements were made possible through truancy? (I)

Dante: *La Vita Nuova*
Petrarch: *Sonnets*
Boccaccio: *The Decameron*

THREE ASPECTS OF RENAISSANCE LOVE

Compare and contrast the meaning of 'Love' for Dante, Petrarch, and Boccaccio.

What role does the loved one play for each? What is the significance of love for the poet? For the world? Compare and contrast briefly Beatrice, Laura, and Fiametta. (III)

Machiavelli: *The Prince*

THE EVILS OF FORTUNE AND THEIR REMEDIES IN MACHIAVELLI

Analyze the treatment of Fortune and man's remedies against its destructiveness in The Prince.

How can Fortune be controlled and to what ends? (II)

Machiavelli: *The Prince*
Plus any history of Italy and the Florentine republic during Machiavelli's lifetime, 1469-1527.

THE JUSTICE OF *The Prince*

Is the reputation of the Machiavellian politics justified?

Consider *The Prince* as a political treatise; reconsider it as the product of a particular political situation, a monument to the new objective method of scholarship developed by the humanists and a foretaste of the attempt to establish universal principles of behavior. (III)

Machiavelli: *The Prince*

MACHIAVELLI ON HUMAN NATURE

Examine the Machiavellian concept of Man in THE PRINCE.

What is man? What is his role in society? What is the role of the politician? How may the ruler accomplish his ends and why? (I)

Machiavelli: *The Prince*
The Mandrake

CALLIMACO: GENIUS OR FOOL?

Compare and contrast the character Callimaco in THE MANDRAKE *with Machiavelli's concept of Man in* THE PRINCE.

Does Callimaco characterize the type of man one sees in *The Prince?* What are the essential differences, if any? What is the significance of this character for Machiavelli? (II)

Castiglione: *The Courtier*

EDUCATIONAL IDEAS IN CASTIGLIONE

Outline the ideals of education in THE COURTIER.

What was the object of education for the author? What is the evidence in this work of the social and intellectual reasons for this ideal? (I)

Castiglione: *The Courtier*
Machiavelli: *The Prince*

THE EVILS OF FORTUNE AND THEIR REMEDIES IN CASTIGLIONE AND MACHIAVELLI

Compare and contrast the treatments of Fortune and man's remedies against its destructiveness in THE PRINCE *and* THE COURTIER.

How could fortune be controlled in each case? To what ends? (III)

Castiglione: *The Courtier*

WOMEN: BEASTS OR ANGELS?

Examine the role of women in society according to Castiglione.

What role does the woman play in *The Courtier?* What is the 'jest?' How should it be used? What is woman's chief virtue? What is the ideal woman? (II)

Rabelais: *Pantagruel*
Gargantua
Castiglione: *The Courtier*

EDUCATIONAL IDEALS IN RABELAIS AND CASTIGLIONE

Compare and contrast the ideals of education in THE COURTIER *and* GARGANTUA *and* PANTAGRUEL.

What were the objects of education for the two

authors? What are the social and intellectual differences between them? What caused this difference? (III)

Rabelais: *Gargantua*
Pantagruel

BANALITY IN RABELAIS

Examine the use of the description of prurient elements of existence in Rabelais.

In what way are these aspects connected to the world beauty under God in Rabelais? (I)

Rabelais: *Gargantua*
Pantagruel

LAUGHTER IS A HUMAN FUNCTION

Explore the use of laughter or humor in GARGANTUA.

What is the significance of laughter for Rabelais? Why did he feel that a good sense of humor was essential? How is laughter used in *Gargantua* and *Pantagruel?* (II)

Rabelais: *Gargantua*
Pantagruel

THE PURPOSE OF LEARNING: RABELAIS

What precisely is the purpose of learning for Rabelais?

What is the object of knowledge? Why? What role does learning play in the intellectual framework of time? (III)

Montaigne: *Essays*

PLEASURE IN MONTAIGNE

Examine Montaigne's treatment of pleasure in the ESSAYS.

What constitutes pleasure? What is its moral quality? Why is it important to Montaigne? (II)

Montaigne: *Essays*

THE PERFECTABILITY OF MAN: MONTAIGNE

Analyze the ideas of man's perfectability in Montaigne.

How far can man be perfected? What are the forces which hinder him from perfection? (III)

Boccaccio: *The Decameron*
Montaigne: *Essays*

WOULD MONTAIGNE HAVE PLEASED BOCCACCIO?

Compare and contrast the treatment of Pleasure in THE DECAMERON *and the* ESSAYS.

What is the moral quality of pleasure for both? Why is it important to both? What is its relation to other aspects of the thought of these two men?
(I, II, III)

Montaigne: *Essays*

"WHAT DO I KNOW?"

How does this quotation embody Montaigne's conclusion to his ESSAYS?

Analyze Montaigne's attitude to human reason and human science. (II, III)

Montaigne: *Essays*

"KNOW THYSELF AS THOU WOULDST KNOW ALL MEN"

Show, with examples, how this is the motto for the ESSAYS *of Montaigne.*

Examine the *Essays* and their content to show this motto. What is Montaigne's concept of the self? What is his attitude toward knowledge, ethics, authority, philosophy? (III)

Cervantes: *Don Quixote*

QUIXOTE: MAN OR SYMBOL?

Analyze the symbolic references of Don Quixote.

Who is Quixote? Why is chivalry treated this way? What evidence in the work is there of idealism? What evidence of vulgar reality? Which of the two does Cervantes prefer? (I)

Cervantes: *Don Quixote*

Quixote AS SATIRE

Analyze DON QUIXOTE *in the framework of satire.*

What is satire? What is its role in the body of literature? Is *Quixote* only a satire? (III)

Cervantes: *Don Quixote*

Quixote AS COMEDY

Analyze the evidence of comedy in Don Quixote.

What is comedy? Does *Quixote* fulfill this definition? Show the elements of slapstick. Is *Quixote* absurd? (II)

Cervantes: *Don Quixote*

QUIXOTE AND SANCHO

Examine the two characters in detail.

What is their mental image of life? What does the difference in their imaginations signify? What is the author's vision of the world as seen through the two characters? What is the Quixotic ideal?
(I, II, III)

De Camoens: *The Luciads*
Homer: *Odyssey*

THE EPIC QUALITY OF *The Luciads*

Examine THE LUCIADS *in terms of the traditional epic.*

Where does the strength of the epic lie? Where are its weaknesses? How does this work compare in stature with Homer? (III)

De Camoens: *The Luciads*

The Luciads

Examine The Luciads *in terms of national and human significance.*

Are there realistic descriptions of the emotions and experiences of the characters? If so, give evidence. How much dependence did the author place on classical machinery and pagan traditions? Does this weaken or strengthen the work? (II, III)

Desiderius Erasmus: *In Praise of Folly*

WHAT IS FOLLY?

Determine the wisdom of Folly as it is presented in Erasmus, In Praise of Folly.

Evaluate the opinions of the book, keeping in mind that it is a fool who speaks them. (II)

Desiderius Erasmus: *In Praise of Folly*

THE NATURAL AND SOCIAL MAN IN ERASMUS

Analyze the author's treatment of these two aspects of man.

How does the author resolve the conflict between man's natural needs and rights and his social obligations? Which aspect does he value more? (III)

French Neo-Classic

Moliere: *Tartuffe*

COMEDY AND TRAGEDY IN *Tartuffe*

Discuss the tragic overtones in Moliere's comedy.

Analyze the comic devices used and investigate the possibility of an underlying tragedy. (II)

Moliere: *That Scoundrel Scapin*

SCAPIN

A study of the style of Moliere.

What is the function of the scoundrel? Analyze the scoundrel's character. What is his significance to Moliere? (III)

Moliere: *The Misanthrope*

REALITY IN *The Misanthrope*

Analyze the work in terms of the author's realistic portrayal of the characters.

Is Alceste an unreasonable hero? What is the character of Célimène? What kind of a man is Oronte? Is Eleante a good woman? What is the character of Arsinoë? (II, III)

Moliere: *The Misanthrope*
Tartuffe

MOLIERE AS SATIRIST

Examine The Misanthrope *and* Tartuffe *from the standpoint of satire.*

What is satire? Does either work fulfill the definition? Are they comic or tragic? What is the nature of the truth they present? Is it universal?
(III)

Moliere: *Tartuffe*

Tartuffe: THE FOLLIES OF HUMAN NATURE

Examine the character of Tartuffe.

What is Tartuffe's effect on the audience? Does the character evoke hatred and bitterness? Why? Give evidence to show the hypocrisy of the character and what this hypocrisy represents. (I, II)

The Works of Moliere

THE ART OF MOLIERE

An analysis of the works of Moliere.

Discuss the sanity of Moliere; his wit and easy grace. Show how Moliere penetrates to the roots of human absurdity; discuss his plays as plays of character. (III)

The Works of Moliere

MOLIERE: THE MORALIST

A discussion of the plays as showing concern with the improvement of manners.

Trace Moliere's castigation of hypocrisy, pretentiousness, dishonesty, excess, folly, perverted values, and injustice in family relationships. Discuss these in the light of the Neo-Classic tendency toward didacticism. (I, II, III)

Corneille: *Le Cid*

THE LACK OF RESOLUTION IN *Le Cid*

Discuss the possibility of a compromise in Le Cid.

Corneille makes his moral very clear throughout the play; yet at the end, the outcome is unclear and a compromise is suggested. Does this weaken the theme of the play? (I)

Corneille: *Le Cid*

THE ROLE OF LOVE IN CORNEILLE

What role does love play in the work of Corneille?

Examine the love of Rodrique and his father; Rodrique and Chimòne. Is love the central conflict? (II)

The Works of Pierre Corneille

CORNEILLE AS A WRITER OF TRAGEDY

Discuss the essential characteristics of tragedy found in Corneille.

Examine the central conflict in his works; what is the function of passion? The function of reason? Discuss the characters as heroic or non-heroic; are they capable of human weakness? Where does the tragedy lie? (III)

Corneille: *Rodogume*
Racine: *Athalie*

A COMPARISON OF CLEOPATRA AND ATHALIE

Analyze the characters in these two plays.

What are the motives of each queen? What function does each serve in the dramatic action? How is each presented? (III)

The Plays of Racine

RACINE AND THE NEO-CLASSIC TRADITION

Examine Racine's plays in terms of the three unities.

What is the functioning plot? Give evidence of the unity of time, action and place in his works. (III)

The Plays of Racine

RACINE AND THE THEME OF LOVE

Examine the role of love in Racine's works.

What function does love play in the works of

Racine? Is it a recurrent theme? What is the role of women? Do they have tragic dignity? How does love affect the plot? (II)

Racine: *Andromaque*
Phèdre

RACINE'S WOMEN

Analyze the characters of Phèdre and Hermions.

How are they presented? How are their emotions presented? What sort of language do they use? What does language and emotion on the part of these women indicate, i.e., what is their stature?
(I)

Voltaire: *Candide*

Candide, MASTERPIECE OF SKEPTICISM

Discuss Candide *in the light of skepticism.*

Distinguish between skepticism and cynicism. Is Voltaire satisfied with the way things were? How does he treat philosophic optimism? What is the salvation? (II, III)

Voltaire: *The English Letters*

VOLTAIRE AND THE FRENCH REVOLUTION

Discuss Voltaire's influence on the unrest which ultimately delivered the French Revolution.

Discuss the differences between "free" England as Voltaire saw it and "oppressed" France. What was Voltaire's attitude toward English philosophy and literature? (III)

FRENCH NEO-CLASSIC 57

Voltaire: *Candide*

Candide, THE ATTACKER

Discuss the subjects which are taken to task in Candide.

What was Voltaire's position on: follies of war; religious persecution; governmental persecution; ambition; man; happiness. (I)

Voltaire: *Candide*

WHO IS PANGLOSS?

Examine the character of Pangloss in detail.

What is Pangloss? What is his philosophy of life? What is the significance of his cure by the Anabaptist? From a religious standpoint, who is Pangloss? (II)

Voltaire: *Candide*

VOLTAIRE'S WOMEN

Examine the role of women in Candide.

What is Voltaire's attitude toward women? How are they presented? Compare and contrast Cunégonde and the old woman. What does woman symbolize? (I)

Voltaire: *Candide*

"CRUSH THE INFAMOUS THING"

Discuss Voltaire's motto in terms of Candide.

Do the characters in *Candide* reflect Voltaire's feelings about superstition and intolerance? How?

How is the problem solved? Show how Voltaire tries to wage war against oppression. Voltaire was a champion for freedom of thought; show how this is reflected in *Candide*. (III)

English Neo-Classic

Sidney: *An Apologeia for Poesie*
Rabelais: *Pantagruel* **and** *Gargantua*

THE PURPOSE OF LEARNING: SIDNEY AND RABELAIS

Compare and contrast the views of the purposes of learning by these authors.

What is the object of knowledge for each author? Why? (II)

Sidney: *Astrophel and Stella*

VARIETY IN SIDNEY'S *Astrophel and Stella*

Using the completely conventional sonnet form and the over-worked theme of unrequited love, Sidney has produced a work of freshness and variety. In what ways is this variety achieved?

Consider the metrics of these sonnets, noting the frequent use of caesura and run-on lines. Pay close attention to the changing stance of the narrator. Compare a sonnet of Sidney to one of Wyatt or Drayton. (III)

Edmund Spenser: "Epithalamion"

THE BLENDING OF PAGAN MYTH WITH CHRISTIAN CEREMONY IN SPENSER'S *"Epithalamion"*

Consider Spenser's application of pagan myth to

the intrinsically Christian sacrament of marriage. How does the poet achieve harmony between these discordant elements?

Compare Spenser's poem to "Epithalamion" written by Catullus. (III)

A. C. Hamilton: *The Structure of Allegory in the Faerie Queene*

THE ALLEGORICAL SIGNIFICANCE OF THE FIRST BOOK OF THE *Faerie Queene*

The first book of the Faerie Queene *works on at least three levels. The narrative is paralleled by an intricate religious and political allegory. Attempt to unravel these various levels of allegorical meaning.*

Carefully review the history of the period from the accession of Queen Elizabeth to the defeat of the Spanish Armada. (III)

Wm. Shakespeare: *Antony and Cleopatra*

RECURRENT IMAGES IN *Antony and Cleopatra*

Trace the imagery of the "horse," "serpent," or "rule" in Antony and Cleopatra. *Assuming that these images take on the significance of symbols, what do they symbolize?*

Discover with whom these various images are recurrently associated. With what countries are these characters associated? (II)

Wm. Shakespeare: *Measure for Measure*
Merchant of Venice

Measure for Measure: A STUDY IN JUSTICE
Contrast the various views of justice presented in this play.

Compare Angelo's sense of justice to the Duke's. In what way does Angelo change during the course of the play? Compare Angelo with Portia's "quality of mercy" speech in *Merchant of Venice*. (II)

John Donne: "Holy Sonnets"
George Herbert: "The Temple"

THE RELIGIOUS EXPERIENCE IN DONNE AND HERBERT

Both Donne and Herbert wrote sacred verses, and yet these poems are very dissimilar. Explore this dissimilarity.

Contrast in each case the narrator's approach to religious experience. Is it one of violence or ease? Assuming a difference of approach, explore the total effect of that difference on the poem as a whole. Is the movement toward tension or relaxation? (II)

The Plays of Jonson and Shirley

SOCIAL COMEDY IN JONSON AND SHIRLEY

Compare and contrast, using a play of both authors, the type of social comedy used by each.

What is the moral perspective of each author? What are the particular social qualities under examination? What are the differences between the societies in which the authors lived? (III)

John Milton: *Paradise Lost*

SATAN AND MANKIND COMPARED

Trace the similarities between the fall of Satan and the fall of man.

What particular aspiration causes Satan to rebel? Can this aspiration be found in Satan's temptation of Eve? What other parallels can you find?
(II)

Virgil: *Aeneid*
Milton: *Paradise Lost*

THE HERO AND FREEDOM

Determine the relationship between heroic action and freedom in both the Aeneid *and* Paradise Lost *and compare your findings.*

Is freedom consonant with heroism in these works? Or is freedom a state of being which the hero rejects? (II)

Jonathan Swift: *A Tale of a Tub*
Lawrence Sterne: *Tristram Shandy*

STERNE'S DEBT TO SWIFT

In what way does the form and style of Tristram Shandy *reflect the form and style of* A Tale of a Tub?

Consider the use of digression. In what way does the narrator's inability to understand figurative language in *Tale of a Tub* suggest the total breakdown of communication in *Tristram Shandy*. (III)

Jonathan Swift: *A Tale of a Tub*

THE RELATION OF TEXT AND DIGRESSION IN
A Tale of a Tub

In the "Apology," the narrator tells us that his purpose is dual. He will satirize the abuses in religion by means of allegory and the abuses in learning by means of digression. What is the relation between the two?

What is the relation between Peter's interpretation of the *Bible* in Section II and the account of modern critics in Section III. Apply the same reasoning to the other chapters of the book. (III)

Alexander Pope: "The Rape of the Lock"

THE POET'S POSITION IN "THE RAPE OF THE LOCK"

Is Pope's attitude toward the world of Belinda wholly satiric?

Search for evidence of Pope's approval of Belinda's world. Within the poem, is there any glimpse into the real world of 18th century England? How is it described? (II)

Henry Fielding: *Tom Jones*

THE ROLE OF THE NARRATOR IN *Tom Jones*

What is the effect of a third person narrative? Is the narrator himself a sort of character in the book?

Compare *Tom Jones* to another 18th century novel using a first person narrative. (Any by Defoe or Richardson would make a good comparison.) (II)

French Romantic

Rousseau: *Discourse on Inequality*

MAN AND SOCIETY: JEAN-JACQUES ROUSSEAU

Examine the role of man in society in the works of Rousseau.

What is the nature of man? Is he corrupt and, if so, how was he corrupted? How does Rousseau propose to solve the problem? (I)

Any of Rousseau's Works

FOUNDATIONS OF ROMANTICISM: JEAN-JACQUES ROUSSEAU

Discuss Rousseau's works as one of the foundations of the Romantic Period.

Examine the style of Rousseau. Show how he violates the Neo-Classic method for clarity; correctness of style, conduct, ideas and social values. (III)

Rousseau: *Collected Works*
Boccaccio: *The Decameron*

THE ROLE OF THE CITY

Compare and contrast the role of the city in Rousseau and Boccaccio.

Examine the attitudes of both authors toward the city. How do they differ? How are they similar? Is the movement toward or away from the city in each? Why? (II)

Rousseau: *Emile*
Sidney: *An Apologeia for Poesie*

THE PURPOSE OF LEARNING: ROUSSEAU AND SIDNEY

Compare and contrast the views of the purposes of learning for both authors.

What is the object of knowledge for each author? Why? What role does learning play in society for each? (II)

Rousseau: *The Social Contract*
Emile

REVOLT AGAINST SOCIAL ORDER

Discuss Rousseau's revolt against the existing social order of his time.

How does Rousseau propose to improve society? What is his attitude toward the relation of evil to society. (II)

Francois-Auguste, Viscount of Chateaubriand: *The Genius of Christianity*

MELANCHOLY: CHATEAUBRIAND

Discuss the preoccupation with the self in Chateaubriand and how it reflects the tenor of the Romantic Period.

What is melancholy? Could it be called pessimism in Chateaubriand? Was this melancholy real or just a pose? (II)

Chateaubriand: *The Genius of Christianity*

THE APPEAL OF RELIGION

Discuss Chateaubriand's attitude toward religion.

Why does Chateaubriand favor Christianity. (I)

Chateaubriand: *Memoirs from Beyond the Tomb*

THE ROLE OF THE SELF: CHATEAUBRIAND AND THE ROMANTICS

Discuss the role of the self, both in the life and the writings of Chateaubriand.

How did this preoccupation with the self come about? Why has Chateaubriand been considered, after Rousseau, the greatest influence on the Romantic Period. (II)

Victor Hugo: *Odes and Ballads*

Odes and Ballads OF VICTOR HUGO

An analysis of the poetic style of Victor Marie Hugo.

What is the overall sentiment of the poems? Some have said that he used a Neo-Classic technique. Is this true? If so, how does one justify this in view of Hugo's Romantic convictions? (II)

Hugo: *The Hunchback of Notre Dame*

BRETON INFLUENCE IN HUGO

Discuss the Breton influence on Hugo as seen in The Hunchback of Notre Dame.

How does the Breton influence affect Hugo's work? Where does it occur most often? (II)

Hugo: *The Hunchback of Notre Dame*

NOTRE-DAME: A MINIATURE OF PARIS

Discuss the role of the cathedral in The Hunchback of Notre-Dame

What does the cathedral represent? Is it the focal point of existence? If so, why? Could this cathedral function in the 20th century as it did in this 15th century setting? (I)

Hugo: *Les Miserables*

HUGO AND THE HEROIC IDEAL

Analyze Hugo's preference for heroic periods and the role of the hero in his work.

What is the purpose of reconstructing the past for Hugo? Is he merely concerned with the historic value or does this recreation serve a better end? What is the role of the hero in *Les Miserables*? How does he resolve his conflict and to what end? (III)

Alexander Dumas, Père:
The Count of Monte Cristo
The Three Musketeers

THE IMPORTANCE OF ALEXANDER DUMAS, PÈRE

An analysis of the style of Alexander Dumas, Père.

Can Dumas be considered a great novelist? Do his works have any distinction of style or characterization? Are they anything more than tales of popular successes? What is his importance? (II)

Dumas: ***The Count of Monte Cristo***

FINANCE IN *The Count of Monte Cristo*

Analyze Dumas' attitude toward finance in The Count of Monte Cristo.

What does Dumas tell us about French society at that time? (I)

German Romantic

Ewald Christian von Kleist: ***Der Frühling (Spring)***

KLEIST: *Spring*

Examine the poem in the light of the Romantic Movement.

What is the central theme of the poem? How does this differ from the Neo-Classic tradition? What does Nature represent to the author? (II)

Kleist: ***The Prince of Homburg***

KLEIST'S CONCEPT OF HONOR

A Study of Kleist's treatment of honor in The Prince of Homburg.

How does honor dictate the behavior of the characters? What does Kleist think of this? When is honor ignored? Why? Is this good or bad? (I)

Lessing: ***Minna von Barnhelm***
Emilia Galotti

LESSING AND THE BOURGEOIS DRAMA

A study of the origins of the bourgeois drama.

Evaluate the role of the bourgeois characters. How does the playwright regard them? (II)

Lessing: *Emilia Galotti*
Kleist: *The Prince of Homburg*

THE CONCEPT OF HONOR: LESSING AND KLEIST

An analysis of the treatment of honor.

What is the significance of honor for both? How does it dictate the lives of the characters? Could this be called fate? (III)

Lessing: *Laokoon*
Hamburgische Dramaturgie
Litteraturbriefe

THE CRITICAL INFLUENCE OF LESSING

A study of Lessing's critical works.

Evaluate Lessing's critical precepts. In what ways are they influential? How important have his ideas been? To what extent are they still important?
(III)

Any literary history of Germany
Herder: *Fragments on the New German Literature*

Sturm Und Drang: A WAVE OF EMOTION

Discuss the Sturm und Drang *(Storm & Stress) Movement.*

The following elements should be considered:
- The influence of the Seven Year War
- The intermediation of the domestic rulers of Germany
- The pulsing youthful literature of this time
- "Nature" and "Strong Emotion" became synonymous
- It was a revolt against any restricting controls (III)

Goethe: *Collected Poems*

THE POETRY OF GOETHE

A critical evaluation of the poetry of Goethe.

What is the poet doing? How does he achieve his goals? What is the relationship of style to content, and what does it signify? (II)

Goethe: *Goetz von Berlichingen*
Egmont

THE THIN AND THE FAT

A study of Goethe's concept of the hero's role in society.

Study the relation of the heroes to their societies in these plays. How does this develop in the course of these plays? What does Goethe think? How does his attitude change? Why? (II)

Goethe: *Faust*
Marlowe: *Doctor Faustus*

COMPARISON OF *Faust* AND *Doctor Faustus*

Compare and contrast the two characters.

Why is one saved and the other damned? What are the authors' attitudes toward the characters and the concept of salvation? What are the differences in pacts? Why? What are the characters' attitudes toward religion, etc.? Why? (III)

Goethe: *The Sorrows of Young Werther*
Herder: *Fragments on the New German Literature*

GÖTZ AND WERTHER

Compare and contrast the two characters, Götz and Werther.

What did each represent? How did they reflect the *Sturm und Drang* sentiment against any uniform restrictions? Which character is most like the *Sturm und Drang* type? (I)

Goethe: *Faust*
Dante: *The Divine Comedy*

Faust AND *The Divine Comedy*

Compare and contrast these two works in terms of style and structure.

Can *Faust* be called an allegory? Why? Is *Faust* an epic? Why? Are the structures tight and objective in both? (III)

Goethe: *Faust*

SYMBOLISM IN *Faust*

Examine the symbols of God and the Devil and how these function in Faust.

How are they presented? What is Goethe's attitude toward both? Can they be considered as the forces which act upon Man? If not, then what are these forces as far as Goethe is concerned? (II)

Goethe: *Egmont*
Schiller: *Maria Stuart*

THE STYLES OF GOETHE AND SCHILLER

What are the significant differences between Goethe and Schiller?

Compare and contrast the two chosen texts. Relate the differences and similarities in style to those in theme. (II)

Johann Christopher Fredrich von Schiller:
The Robbers
Wallenstein
William Tell

SCHILLER AS A RHAPSODIST

Examine the basic motifs of these three works: The Robbers, Wallenstein, *and* William Tell.

Trace the themes of human aspiration, yearning for the ideal, and yearning for freedom in any or all of these works. (III)

Heinrich Heine: *Collected Poems*

LOVE IN THE WORKS OF HEINRICH HEINE

Discuss in detail the various attitudes of the author toward love.

Using several poems, indicate the various mood changes which are characteristic of Heine: from pathos and tenderness to sharp sarcasm and pungent wit. How is love presented? Would you say that Heine is sentimental? (II)

English Romantic

John Keats: "La Belle Dame Sans Merci"
"Fall of Hyperion"
"Eve of St. Agnes"
"Ode to Psyche"

THE USE OF "DREAM" IN KEATS

Trace the recurring use of "dream" in Keats' poetry.

In what way does the use of dream reflect upon Keats' attempt to distinguish illusion from reality in his poetry? (III)

John Keats: "Ode on a Grecian Urn"
"Ode to Autumn"

FROZEN MOTION IN "ODE ON A GRECIAN URN" AND "ODE TO AUTUMN"

Discover the nature and meaning of Keats' perception of motion held in momentary stasis. What is the meaning of such a concept?

Examine images and language for the representations of frozen motion. (III)

John Keats: "Eve of St. Agnes"
"La Belle Dame Sans Merci"

MADELINE AND THE KNIGHT AT ARMS COMPARED

In what respect are Madeline and the Knight at Arms "hoodwinked dreamers?"

How is the Knight's situation at the end of "La Belle Dame" similar to Madeline's position at the end of "Eve of St. Agnes"? How do both characters persist in a relation with something that is not altogether real? (III)

John Keats: "Hyperion"
John Milton: *Paradise Lost*

KEATS' DEBT TO MILTON IN "HYPERION"

How does Keats' "Hyperion" reflect the influence of Milton's Paradise Lost?

Compare the events of "Hyperion" to the events in the first two books of *Paradise Lost*. To what degree does Keats affect the style of Milton? (II)

Samuel Coleridge: "Frost at Midnight"

SILENCE IN "FROST AT MIDNIGHT"

Describe the meaning and use of silence in the poem.

What does the silence provoke in the mind of the poet? How does the poet experience the world around him? (II)

Samuel Coleridge: "The Rime of the Ancient Mariner"
Lord Byron: "Childe Harold"

GUILT IN "THE RIME OF THE ANCIENT MARINER" AND "CHILDE HAROLD"

Examine these poems and compare and contrast their treatments of guilt.

What are the thoughts of the characters in each poem? How does imagery reflect a state of mind? (II)

Coleridge: "The Rime of the Ancient Mariner"

THE RELATION OF THE MARGINALIA TO THE TEXT IN "THE RIME OF THE ANCIENT MARINER"

A discussion of the function of the marginal commentary in Coleridge's poem.

Do you believe that the marginalia are only present for the sake of form? Are they irrelevant to our understanding of the poem? If not, how do they aid it? How do they alter our reaction from what it might be without them? Why do you believe Coleridge used marginalia instead of trying to incorporate such comments into the poem or ignoring them altogether? (III)

William Wordsworth: "Mutability"
Percy Bysshe Shelley: "Mutability"

MUTABILITY

Compare and contrast the poems on this subject by Shelley and Wordsworth for theme and metaphor.

How do the poets differ in their treatment of the theme and in their mode of perception? (II)

William Wordsworth: "London, 1802"
William Blake: "London"

WORDSWORTH'S "LONDON, 1802" AND BLAKE'S "LONDON"

Compare and contrast the two views of the city and its life.

Examine theme and imagery in these two poems and show how they are related. (I)

ENGLISH ROMANTIC

Shelley: "The Sensitive Plant"

STAR IMAGERY IN "THE SENSITIVE PLANT"

Keeping in mind the significance of the star in "Adonais," trace the use of star imagery in "The Sensitive Plant."

In the Adonis myth, Adonis is transformed into a flower. In Shelley's "Adonais," the hero is transformed into a flower. In "The Sensitive Plant," how are flowers metaphorically considered as the stars of this world? (II)

Shelley: "Mont Blanc"

POWER IN "MONT BLANC"

What does Shelley mean in "Mont Blanc" when he says, "Mont Blanc yet gleams on high;—the Power is there"?

Considering "power" as "ultimate cause," how does the poem embody Shelley's concept of the meaning of reality as expressed in the *Speculations on Metaphysics*? (III)

Shelley: "Adonais"

MOISTURE AND LIGHT IN "ADONAIS"

Trace the use of light and moisture images in Shelley's "Adonais."

Do these two images take on the significance of symbols? Considering light and moisture as symbols of life and death respectively, how is the poem enriched? (II)

Blake: "The Marriage of Heaven and Hell"

BLAKEAN DIALECTIC

A discussion of Blake's "The Marriage of Heaven and Hell."

Examine how Blake inverts traditional moral values, re-defines "good" and "evil" and praises evil while decrying good. Point out the satirical aspect of this process. Does Blake mean us to stop at his re-definition, or does he point the way to a final synthesis and resolution of these concepts of "good" and "evil"? If the latter, suggest the type of moral concepts toward which he leads us. (III)

Blake: "The Clod and the Pebble"
"The Garden of Love"

"THE CLOD AND THE PEBBLE" AND "THE GARDEN OF LOVE

Discuss and compare the definitions of love in these two poems. In each, what is the view of innocence and of experience? What is the effect of the irresolution of both themes in the poems?

Read the poems carefully and decide where the source of repression lies. (I)

Blake: "Songs of Experience"
Wordsworth: "Lucy Poems"

"SONGS OF EXPERIENCE" AND THE "LUCY POEMS"

Compare these two sequences as presentations of reality.

Examine the use of setting and symbol in each case. Which is more abstract? Which more naturalistic? Which more realistic? (III)

Shelley: "Ode to the West Wind"
Keats: "Ode to a Nightingale"

"Ode to the West Wind" and "Ode to a Nightingale"

Compare these poems in terms of imagery, meter, and type of sympathetic reaction to a naturalistic occurrence.

How do the imagery and meter bear out the differences in the poets' reactions? Which poet seems to become more closely the object contemplated?

(III)

The Poetry of Shelley and Keats

Realism in Shelley and Keats

Choose a poem by each author and discuss the uses of naturalistic detail in each.

How is realism used in the poetic framework? Which poet is more realistic? (III)

Selected Poetry of Blake, Wordsworth, Keats, Shelley

Romantic Poets, Their Repudiation of Christianity

Blake, Wordsworth, Shelley, Keats all found it necessary to repudiate Christianity. Formulate an explanation of this general trend.

How do these poets base their work on sensual experience? In what way is this incompatible with Christian doctrine? Each of these poets created his own system in substitution for the Christian myth. How do their own private systems parallel or diverge from the Christian church? (III)

French Realism

Stendhal: *The Red and the Black*
The Charterhouse of Parma

STENDHAL'S WOMEN

A study of the women in The Red and the Black *and* The Charterhouse of Parma.

How are women presented? What is the author's attitude? Compare and contrast Mathilde and Mme. de Rênal. What are the essential differences? How do these women compare with the women in *The Charterhouse*? (II)

Stendhal: *The Red and the Black*

JULIEN SOREL—MODERN HERO?

Examine the character of Julien Sorel in The Red and the Black.

What are Sorel's qualities? Is he at any time presented as heroic? How does he compare with the traditional concept of hero? Would Sorel be considered a hero in the 20th century? (II)

Stendhal: *The Red and the Black*
The Charterhouse of Parma

STENDHAL'S RELIGION

An analysis of the role of the clergy in the works of Stendhal.

How is the clergy presented? What does the author feel about the power of the clergy? (III)

Guy de Maupassant: *Collected Short Stories*

GUY DE MAUPASSANT: NATURALIST OR REALIST?

Examine several of the short stories in the light of the Naturalistic and Realistic movements.

Which are Realistic? Which are Naturalistic? Which style predominates? (II)

Scandinavian Realism

Nietzsche: *Thus Spoke Zarathustra*
The Birth of Tragedy and the Genealogy of Morals

Strindberg: *Letters to Nietzsche*
The Father
The Stronger
To Damascus
Ghost Sonata

NIETZSCHE'S INFLUENCE ON STRINDBERG

A study of how Strindberg employed the ideas of Nietzsche.

Attempt to comprehend the broad outlines of Nietzsche's thought. Approach the body of Strindberg's work with these outlines firmly in mind. Which of Nietzsche's ideas does Strindberg reject? Why? How does he modify the ideas which he uses? (III)

Strindberg: *The Stronger*
The Father
Miss Julie

THE NATURALISTIC STRINDBERG

An investigation of the theories and characteristics that made Strindberg the only successful Naturalistic dramatist.

Examine Strindberg's Naturalistic works to determine the exact manner in which they adhere to the tenets of Naturalism. With this information, examine the methods which he used to accomplish his purposes. (II)

Strindberg: *Son of a Servant*
The Father
The Stronger
Miss Julie
A Dream Play
The Ghost Sonata

STRINDBERG'S ARTISTIC DEVELOPMENT

Analyze Strindberg's major works in chronological order, and attempt to determine the nature of the major trends and developments. (II)

Strindberg: *The Ghost Sonata*
A Dream Play
To Damascus

THE EXPRESSIONISTIC STRINDBERG

A study of the distinguishing characteristics of Strindberg's expressionistic works.

An analysis and comparison of the recurring characteristics in Strindberg's major expressionistic plays. (II)

Ibsen: *Peer Gynt*
Ghosts
Pillars of the Community
Julian the Apostate

IBSEN, THE ORIGINATOR OF PSYCHOLOGICAL DRAMA

Ibsen has been called the originator of psychological drama. What does this mean, and is it true?

How explicit is the use of psychology in Ibsen? Is it merely the use of "real" motives, or is it a conscious exploration of the workings of the mind? How new is it? (II)

Ibsen: *Peer Gynt*

THE QUESTION OF PEER GYNT

An attempt to determine whether or not Ibsen's Peer Gynt *is an expressionistic drama.*

Analyze the text in terms of the major characteristics of expressionistic drama, and attempt to determine if the expressionistic techniques that Ibsen employs are used for the reasons that the expressionists were to have. (II)

Ibsen: *Ghosts*
Pillars of the Community
The Wild Duck
Hedda Gabler

THE SOCIAL AND PSYCHOLOGICAL EFFECTS OF TRUTH IN IBSEN

An investigation of the various after effects of the revelation of truth in Ibsen's works.

Analyze Ibsen's works to discover the truth of

each situation. Determine the effects of this truth becoming known to the protagonists. At this point, several alternate approaches are possible: the development could be traced; a generalized position determined; etc. (I)

Ibsen: *The Wild Duck*

MARRIAGE IN *The Wild Duck*

Analyze the treatment of marriage in the play.

How does the author regard marriage? How does marriage affect the dramatic action? What do the characters think of marriage? (I)

Ibsen: *The Wild Duck*

THE CHARACTER OF THE YOUNG GIRL IN *The Wild Duck*

Examine the characterization and role of the young girl in the play.

What is the significance of the young girl in the play? How does she affect the dramatic action? (I)

Ibsen: *The Enemy of the People*

IRONY IN IBSEN

Discuss the irony in The Enemy of the People.

Is the title ironic? Who is the real enemy of the people? Why? (II)

Post-Romantic Germany

Gerhard Hauptman: *Before Sunrise*

HUMAN DESTINY IN GERHARD HAUPTMAN

Examine the causes of human destiny in the plays of Hauptman.

What are the determinants of human destiny for the author? What is the author's attitude toward environment? How does environment affect the dramatic action? (II)

Hauptman: *Before Sunrise*
The Weavers

THE ROLE OF SOCIETY IN THE PLAYS OF GERHARD HAUPTMAN

Discuss the author's attitude toward society.

How is society depicted? What is essentially wrong with it? Is society just? (III)

Hauptman: *The Sunken Bell*

The Sunken Bell: DUTY OR DESIRE

Analyze the play with these themes in mind.

What is Heinrich's basic motivation? How does the author present the questions of social responsibility and individual yearning? What is the author's attitude toward both? (II)

The Poems of Rainer Maria Rilke

LOVE AND DEATH IN THE POETRY OF RILKE

Discuss the poet's use of both themes.

How does Rilke present each? Is he afraid of either one? How does his feeling affect the poetry? (III)

Rilke: Poems

THE EXTERNAL WORLD

Discuss the use of externals in the poetry of Rilke.

How are externals used? What function do they perform? Do you feel that there is a sense of the mystical in the externalization of the essence of the world? (II)

Rilke: *The Love and Death of Ensign Christopher Rilke*

EQUINE IMAGERY IN RILKE

An analysis of the use of equine images by Rilke in The Love and Death of Ensign Christopher Rilke.

Develop a theory to account for the use of equine imagery by this poet. What is the effect of the theme on setting and how does the setting affect the use of equine imagery? (I)

Victorian England

George Eliot: *The Mill on the Floss*

FATE IN *The Mill on the Floss*

How does an overriding destiny act on the characters in The Mill on the Floss?

In what ways are the characters prisoners within themselves? How does chance or coincidence influence their lives? How is the river used as a symbol of the inexorable process of existence? (II)

Charles Dickens: *Hard Times*
Feodor Dostoevski: *Crime and Punishment*

Dickensian Influence in Dostoevski

Show the relationship between the writings of Dickens and Dostoevski.

Study Dickens' portrayal of an industrialized society. How does Dostoevski show the influence of Dickens' attitude and description? (II)

Charles Dickens: *Bleak House*

The Function of Setting in *Bleak House*

How does the setting contribute to Dickens' Bleak House *and help to convey the meaning of the book?*

Consider the main settings of the book, particularly the fog, Chancery, and the Dedlock's house. How does their description aid in conveying either a feeling or a message? How does the fog function as the central symbol of the book? Pay particular attention to the chapters narrated by Dickens himself. (II)

Thomas Hardy: *Far From the Madding Crowd*
T. S. Eliot: *After Strange Gods*

The Meaning of Landscape in *Far From the Madding Crowd*

Would you agree with T. S. Eliot that landscape for Hardy simply "lends itself to the author's mood?" Or does it have a significance of its own?

Look closely at passages where the landscape is described; what effect does it have on the characters? (III)

Thomas Hardy: *The Return of the Native*
The Mayor of Casterbridge
Tess of the D'Ubervilles

The Use of the Villagers As Chorus in Hardy

A discussion of how Hardy employs the background figures—natives of villages, etc.—in his novels.

Most of the scenes in Hardy are conducted against a backdrop of minor village figures who comment frequently on the action. How do they assume a kind of choric function? Do they have a collective wisdom which is borne out by the plot? How does Hardy use them to introduce irony? How does their commentary interact with our response to the main action? (II)

Thomas Hardy: *Tess of the D'Ubervilles*

The Presence of the Author in *Tess of the D'Ubervilles*

Discuss the extent of the author's voice and opinions in the novel.

Why does the author intrude his tone and judgments into the course of the narrative? How does this affect the representation of reality? What can you tell of Hardy's temperament and personality from the novel? (II)

Thomas Hardy: "Neutral Tones"

Title and Content of "Neutral Tones"

A discussion of Hardy's poem "Neutral Tones," in terms of its title.

In what ways does the poem itself consist of

"neutral tones?" How do the images fulfill this description? The syntax? The theme of the poem?
(II)

Emily Brontë: *Wuthering Heights*

POETRY AND REALISM IN *Wuthering Heights*

What are the poetic qualities of the novel? How is it realistic? Does the poetry in the book jeopardize its credibility, or does it force the reader to enter another realm of "realism?"

What effect does description have in the book? Do you believe in the appearances of visions in the book? Are the passionate characters realistic?
(III)

Robert Browning: *The Statue and the Bust*
Matthew Arnold: *Palladium*

The Statue and the Bust AND *Palladium*

Compare and contrast theme, metaphor, and texture in these poems.

What is each poem about? How does the author of each use language and rhythm to say what he means?
(II)

William Thackeray: *Vanity Fair*

Vanity Fair: HEROISM IN THE UNHEROIC NOVEL

Vanity Fair *is a novel without a hero. What qualities come closest to becoming heroic in the context of the novel?*

Examine the main characters closely. Decide what the criteria for heroism in the novel might be, and what character(s) fulfills them best.
(II)

Alfred Tennyson: "Oenone"

"OENONE," RICH IN POETIC LANDSCAPE OR PHILOSOPHICAL CONTENT?

Decide whether the poem is largely artificial or seriously didactic.

Examine the relation of description to doctrine, in terms of relative length and apparent attention to manner of expression. (III)

John Keats: "Ode to a Nightingale"
Alfred Tennyson: "The Lotus-Eaters"

THE POET'S ATTITUDE TOWARD DEATH: KEATS'S "ODE TO A NIGHTINGALE" AND TENNYSON'S "THE LOTUS-EATERS"

In each case, find what produces the longing for death. What is the precise nature of the death in each case?

Examine the imagery of each poem, paying attention to all poetic effects. (III)

Matthew Arnold: "Isolation. To Marguerite"
"The Buried Life"
"The Scholar Gypsy"
"Thyrsis"
"Dover Beach"

ARNOLD'S VIEW OF LIFE

Examination of selected poems of Arnold to define his view of the human condition.

Consider the poems listed above in arriving at a statement of Arnold's philosophy. Try to make a balanced picture, including both his hope and his despair. (II)

Jane Austen: *Pride and Prejudice*

HOW SATIRE IS CONVEYED IN *Pride and Prejudice*

A study of Austen's satirical devices.

How does Austen make us feel that some (or all) of her characters are being undercut and satirized? How does she get us to laugh at them or scorn them? What in their speech indicates their shortcomings? What in their actions? (II)

Russia—19th Century

Alexander Pushkin: *Boris Godunov*
Shakespeare: *Macbeth*
            Henry IV

BORIS GODUNOV: 19TH CENTURY, *Macbeth* AND *Henry IV*

Compare and contrast the three plays.

What are the essential differences in the three characters? (III)

Pushkin: *Eugene Onyegin*
Byron: *Don Juan*
        Beppo

THE BYRONIC INFLUENCE ON PUSHKIN

Discuss the influence of Byron on Pushkin.

Examine *Onyegin*. Does Byron, in your opinion, seem to have an influence on Pushkin in this poem? How, if at all, does Byron's influence affect the style of the poem? (II)

Nicolai Gogol: *Collected Works*

GOGOL: ROMANTIC OR REALIST?

Discuss the work of Gogol with these two schools in mind.

Which does Gogol belong to? Is it the subject matter which leads you to this conclusion? Is it the style? Why? (III)

Nicolai Gogol: *Dead Souls*

Dead Souls—WHO ARE THEY

Analyze the 'souls' of this novel in terms of their social significance.

Who are the dead souls? What is their significance for Gogol? How are they presented? Is this satire? (I)

Gogol: *Dead Souls*

Dead Souls: PITY OR CONTEMPT?

Discuss the author's attitude toward society, especially the middle to lower classes.

What is Gogol's attitude toward provincial society? How does he see the commoner? Is there social suffering? How does Gogol treat the subject, comically or satirically? (II)

Ivan Turgenev: *Fathers and Sons*

TURGENEV AND NIHILISM

An examination of the philosophy of Fathers and Sons.

It has been said that Turgenev may have invented the word "nihilism." Examine the novel and its character, Bazarov, in view of this statement. Is Bazarov's philosophy nihilistic? (III)

Feodor Dostoevski: *Crime and Punishment*

"Suffering" in *Crime and Punishment*

Discuss the role of "suffering" in Crime and Punishment.

What is the author's attitude toward suffering? What is its function? Is this a Christian attitude? —What are the results of the suffering? Can these results be achieved in any other way? (I)

Dostoevski: *The Idiot*

Prince Myshkin: Hero or Anti-Hero

Examine the character of Myshkin in detail.

What does he represent? What is his relationship to society? What, in your opinion, was the reasoning behind the author's creation of this character as a clumsy epileptic? (II)

Dostoevski: *The Brothers Karamazov*

Good and Evil in Karamazov

Discuss good and evil and their role in the novel.

Analyze each character; where does each fit in the scale of good and evil? What is the author's attitude toward good and evil? (II)

Beaumarchais: *The Marriage of Figaro*
Tolstoy: *Anna Karenina*

SPOKESMEN FOR THEIR COUNTRY

In what ways did both Beaumarchais and Tolstoy foresee the revolutions in France and Russia?

Compare and contrast the social comments made by Beaumarchais and Tolstoy. Analyze the techniques used by each. (II)

Tolstoy: *War and Peace*

THE INTENTION OF *War and Peace*

What are the author's primary purposes in writing this novel? What does Tolstoy believe causes war—a basic defect in man; political, social, and economic trends; class-structured societies?

Who are the main characters? How do they typify the attitudes and reactions of the upper classes toward war? Does war illuminate character?

(III)

Tolstoy: *War and Peace*

THE STYLE OF TOLSTOY

Examine the style of Tolstoy in War and Peace.

Does the novel have the traditional unity of earlier novels? What is the quality of the narrative? Is it stable? (III)

Anton Chekhov: *Ward N6*
Peasants
The Sea Gull
The Three Sisters
The Cherry Orchard

THE MOOD OF CHEKHOV'S WRITING—SOCIALLY OR INTELLECTUALLY DETERMINED?

Consider the mood of Chekhov's writings to attempt to determine if it is the result of the social situation or of Chekhov's philosophical commitments.

To what extent do you feel that the mood of Chekhov's writing was determined by his social environment—reflecting the worst years of Alexander III's reign? To what extent was the mood due to his general convictions about the constants of human nature? (III)

Anton Chekhov: *The Black Monk*
The Dreary Story
The Three Sisters
The Man in a Case
The Grasshopper
Yonych

CHEKHOV'S CHARACTERS

Analyze the characters that Chekhov created in these stories to determine what features they share. What do their shared characteristics reflect?

Through his characterization, what does Chekhov say about the nature of man? About the nature of Russian society at the time? (I)

Anton Chekhov: *Assorted Short Stories*

THE AMORALITY OF CHEKHOV

Many critics, especially Chekhov's contemporaries, have taken him to task for his "failure" to pass moral judgment on the acts and words of the characters in his stories. Study his short stories to attempt to determine what, if any, is the purpose of this noncommitment.

Is Chekhov really failing to pass moral judgment on his characters' actions? If so, why? Is this a literary device or an intellectual stand? How did his contemporaries in Russian literature express their moral judgments? (II)

Anton Chekhov: *The Three Sisters*
The Cherry Orchard
The Betrothed

OPTIMISM IN CHEKHOV

Analyze these works in regard to the optimistic view of society that Chekhov held.

What did Chekhov see as the future of Russian society? How does he express this? Does his optimism encompass human nature as well? (I)

France—19th Century

Charles Beaudelaire: *The Flowers of Evil*

THE IMMANENCE OF EVIL

A study of the concept of evil in Beaudelaire's poetry.

Analyze and discuss Beaudelaire's attitude toward evil as presented in *The Flowers of Evil*. (I)

The Poetry of Beaudelaire

THE INFLUENCE OF BEAUDELAIRE

Discuss Beaudelaire and the Symbolist Movement.

What is the Symbolist Movement. Why is Beaudelaire considered the founder of this movement? Compare the style of Beaudelaire with other Symbolists such as Verlaine, Rimbaud, Mallarmè.

(III)

Beaudelaire: *Flowers of Evil*

BEAUDELAIRE AND THE GROTESQUE

Discuss Flowers of Evil *for their grotesque quality.*

What is it about these poems that makes them grotesque? What is the poet's intention? How does this quality affect poetic style? (II)

C. F. MacIntyre: The French Symbolist Poetry

"MUSIC ABOVE EVERYTHING"

Examine the French Symbolist style with reference to the above quote.

What were the Symbolists striving for? Did they achieve it and if so, how? Compare and contrast any two Symbolist poets. (III)

Gide: *Paludes*
Mallarmè: *Choice of Poetry*

STERILITY IN THE WORKS OF GIDE AND MALLARMÈ

A comparison of the theme of sterility as seen in Mallarmè's poetry and Paludes *by Gide.*

Analyze the attitudes of Mallarmè and Gide toward this theme, and the techniques used. (II)

America—Colonial Period to the 20th Century

Washington Irving: *The Works of Washington Irving*

WASHINGTON IRVING AS A ROMANTIC

Show that the later tales and legends of Irving are similar in attitude to the Romantic Literature of the Nineteenth Century.

Analyze the sentiment evoked in these stories for the bucolic life Irving describes. How does the use of folklore and local legend contribute to the mood of these tales? (I)

Washington Irving: *The Sketchbook*

THE ART OF DESCRIPTION: IRVING'S *Sketchbook*

In this collection of unrelated vignettes, Irving makes exciting reading of rather ordinary events and places. What are the secrets of his art of description?

Study his choice of words, his phrasing, his pace and other elements of style. What makes his language excel? (II)

Joseph Conrad: *Lord Jim*

ETHICS IN *Lord Jim*

A discussion of Conrad's view of right action in this novel.

What exactly is Jim's failing? Where does he go wrong? Is it the code within which he lives that condemns him, or would anyone condemn his

actions? Does he do penance for his deeds? Is he in any way redeemed? Where do you believe Conrad stands on the moral issues of the book?
(II)

Joseph Conrad: *The Nigger of Narcissus*

MORALITY IN *The Nigger of Narcissus*

A discussion of Conrad's view of right action in this story.

The basic cause of conflict and action in the story is the central character, particularly in the climactic store scene. Is it right for the men to give him so much sympathy and aid when this endangers the ship as a whole? How does Conrad resolve this conflict of situation with basic Christian ethics? (II)

Joseph Conrad: *Nostromo*

TRAGIC IRONY IN *Nostromo*

How does Nostromo's nature and the forces acting upon him finally combine to place him in an inescapably tragic situation?

Consider the principles on which Nostromo lives his life and the role that is forced upon him in the events of the book. (II)

Henry Adams: *The Education of Henry Adams*

WAS HENRY ADAMS EDUCATED?

Did Henry Adams learn anything which broadened his 19th Century Bostonian outlook sufficiently to cope with the coming century?

Define education by suggesting goals. Did Adams achieve these goals? (II)

Stephen Crane: "Voyages"

THE USE OF THE JOURNEY IN "VOYAGES"

Describe the nature of the journey, actual and metaphysical, in this poem.

Examine the theme in terms of metaphor and texture. (III)

Stephen Crane: *The Red Badge of Courage*
The Open Boat
William Carlos Williams: *The Poetry of Crane*
Kenneth Rexroth: *Poems From the Chinese*

CRANE'S PROSE AS IMAGIST POETRY

Point out the elements in Crane's prose which resemble Imagist poetry in style and technique. How does this affect his prose work?

Read closely the descriptive passages of *The Red Badge of Courage*, *The Open Boat*, or other Crane works. Compare them to his own poetry or to that of other poets of the Imagist school. What effect do such poetic usages have on his work as a whole (particularly in *The Red Badge of Courage*)?

(III)

Ralph Waldo Emerson: *Poetical Works*

THE PHILOSOPHICAL METAPHOR IN THE POETRY OF EMERSON

Demonstrate Emerson's repeated use of certain types of symbols and metaphors from nature, and how the character of these metaphors is suited to the doctrines of his poetry.

What images do you find repeated in Emerson's

poetry? What natural forces do these images suggest? How are these forces related to Emerson's philosophy? (II)

Ralph Waldo Emerson: *Nature*
Henry David Thoreau: *Walden*

THE LYRIC AND PHILOSOPHIC SPIRITS: TWO APPROACHES TO TRANSCENDENTALISM

Differentiate between the spirits inherent in the writings of Thoreau and Emerson.

Contrast the styles and levels of approach to the Transcendentalist doctrine of these two authors. How are these approaches linked? (II)

Ralph Waldo Emerson: *Nature*
The American Scholar

MIND OVER MATTER: THE EMERSONIAN REVOLUTION

Show the way in which the philosophy of Emerson departs from the previous rationalism of his earlier writings.

What does Emerson proclaim as the relation of spirit and reason? With what specific problems is he most greatly concerned? Analyze his views of such concepts as beauty and God in terms of such forces as Utilitarianism, Neo-Classicism, and Calvinism. (II)

Nathaniel Hawthorne: *The Scarlet Letter*

CRIME AND PUNISHMENT IN *The Scarlet Letter*

A discussion of Hester Prynne's adultery in the context of the moral atmosphere of her community.

Use of personality study to suggest how Hester's values compared with those of her time and how any differences bear on the effect of the punishment. (III)

Nathaniel Hawthorne: *The Scarlet Letter*

The Scarlet Letter: SPIRITUAL TRANSMOGRIFICATION OF SUPPORTING CHARACTERS

Show how Hawthorne uses the characters of Pearl and Roger Chillingsworth to personify the forces portrayed in the novel.

How does each character take on a supernatural aspect? How does the sin of Hester and Dimmesdale create this aspect? What is revealed in the different fates of Pearl and Chillingsworth? (III)

Nathaniel Hawthorne: *Twice-Told Tales*

THE DUALITY OF IDENTITY IN *Twice-Told Tales*

Show that the characters in Hawthorne's Twice-Told Tales *often recognize forces within their existence without being able to control them.*

Study several characters who are given a degree of self-understanding, such as Ethan Brand, Parson Hooper, or Goodman Brown. How is this understanding still not able to save? (II)

Nathaniel Hawthorne: *The Prophetic Pictures*
The Artist of the Beautiful

THE MORAL CONSCIOUSNESS OF ART IN *The Prophetic Pictures* AND *The Artist of the Beautiful*

How does art, as seen by Hawthorne in these stories, become an expression of a moral consistency?

How in both stories are the pictures "prophetic?" In what way can this element of prophecy be explained by Hawthorne's concept of the nature of man? (II)

Henry Wadsworth Longfellow: *Poetical Works*

THE SORROWS OF PROMETHEUS: LONGFELLOW'S VISION OF THE POET

Analyze Longfellow's consideration of the suffering of the poet, his struggle to perceive, and the reward of his vision.

Study such poems dealing with the poet's task, such as "Prometheus," "Morituri Salutamus," and those dealing with particular poets. (II)

Herman Melville: *Moby Dick*
Mark Twain: *Huckleberry Finn*

THE ROMANCE OF ESCAPE: *Moby Dick* AND *Huckleberry Finn*

Compare the relation of Ishmael and Queequeg and their attitude toward their journey with that of Huck Finn and Jim.

What do Huck Finn and Ishmael have in common in their background? What is the reason of each for their journey? How does the racial difference of Queequeg and Jim enhance the romance and also add depth of human understanding to Ishmael and Huck? (II)

William Shakespeare: *Macbeth*
Herman Melville: *Moby Dick*

AHAB AND MACBETH: EVIL, HEROISM, AND TRAGEDY

Compare the consciousness, actions, and fate of Ahab with that of Macbeth.

To what extent are both characters conscious of their evil and the inevitability of their doom? How is their decision to pursue their ways and confront their doom heroic? Study the role of conscience in each character. (II)

The Works of Melville, Emerson and Thoreau

THE INTRODUCTION OF NATURAL EVIL: MELVILLE VS. EMERSON AND THOREAU

Show that Melville introduces into the Transcendentalist ideal of natural order and the independence of Man's spirit the recognition of forces unfriendly to Man's happiness and success.

Show how Melville portrays the ambivalent forces of Nature. Do Emerson and Thoreau ever directly confront this issue? Contrast Thoreau's view of poverty with Melville's. (II)

Nathaniel Hawthorne: *Rappuccini's Daughter*
The House of the Seven Gables
Herman Melville: *Moby Dick*

A DARKER ANGEL: THE VISION OF HAWTHORNE AND MELVILLE

Show that the presence of Hawthorne and Melville on the scene of American literature introduced a view of life which revealed man's despair.

Study the overwhelming presence of sin and evil in the works of both writers. How does their shared view of the isolation of man contrast with previous views of life? (II)

Herman Melville: *The Confidence Man*

SATIRE IN *The Confidence Man*

Study the extent and purpose of Melville's satire in this novel.

What characteristics does Melville satirize? What elements inherent in human life does this satire show? How does the struggle lead to a meaningful existence in the presence of these elements?
(II)

Herman Melville: *Billy Budd*

THE CRUCIFIXION OF BILLY BUDD

Study Billy Budd as a Christ-figure.

Consider Billy Budd as a portrayal of innocent goodness and a victim of evil. How may the slaying of Claggart be reconciled with this concept? Study Melville's description of the execution and the final words of Billy. Is "God Bless Captain Vere" a Christ-like act of forgiveness or an acceptance of the judgment of Captain Vere?
(II)

Ralph Waldo Emerson: "Give All to Love" "Love"

LOVE AND "SELF-RELIANCE"

Fit Emerson's conception of love into his doctrine of the independent spirit.

What would Emerson state as the metaphysical basis for love? How is the idea of freedom in love, as expressed in "Give All to Love," compatible with Emerson's concept of individuality?

(II)

Ralph Waldo Emerson: *Poetical Works*

BREAKING THE WALLS OF FORM: EMERSON'S POETRY

Show how the poetry of Emerson reveals the beginning of an attempt by poets to escape the restrictions of style and form in the attainment of expression.

How are Emerson's diction, meter, and form in such poems as "Monadnoc," "Give All to Love," and "Threnody" conscious departures from poetic traditions? What effect is thus created? How is this trend continued after Emerson into modern poetry?

(II)

Killis Compbell (ed.): *The Poems of Edgar Allan Poe*
Edward H. Davidson: *Poe: A Critical Study*

POE: AN AMERICAN ROMANTIC

View the poetry of Poe in the light of the outlook of the Romantic Movement in poetry.

Compare Poe's concept of the poet with that of the Romantics. To what extent are Neo-Platonic concepts inherent in both Poe and the Romantics? Show how Poe's understanding of "truth" and "beauty" compares with that of the Romantic poets.

(III)

Edgar Allan Poe: *The Collected Stories of Poe*

THE ELEMENT OF TERROR IN POE

A discussion of Poe's stories as horror stories.

Use examples from several of the short stories to demonstrate the techniques used by Poe to create an atmosphere of suspense and terror, mentioning the problem of maintaining credibility.   (II)

Henry David Thoreau: *Walden*

RELIGIOUS INFLUENCES IN *Walden*

Study the presence and influences of religious doctrines in Thoreau's account of his sojourn at Walden Pond.

How does the nature of Thoreau's retreat manifest Christian overtones? What ideas drawn from nature does he compare with the doctrines of various religions? What is the influence of Hindu asceticism on Thoreau's philosophy?   (II)

Henry David Thoreau: "Smoke" "A Winter Walk"

A TRANSITION OF SYMBOLS IN THOREAU

Compare the associations with the image of smoke in Thoreau's poem, "Smoke," and in the similar poem contained in the essay, "A Winter Walk."

In both poems, smoke becomes a symbol of a presence of Man in Nature. How does Thoreau's feeling regarding this presence change between the two poems?   (II)

Henry David Thoreau: *Walden*

THOREAU'S REFLECTIONS IN "THE PONDS"

Show that the chapter in Walden concerned with "The Ponds" is the culmination and summary of Thoreau's philosophy.

How do Thoreau's various references to the ponds' beauty in terms of both heaven and earth, spirit and existence, reveal the ponds as emblems of proper life? (II)

Mark Twain: *The Celebrated Jumping Frog of Calaveras County*

HUMOROUS EFFECTS IN *The Celebrated Jumping Frog of Calaveras County*

A discussion of why this Twain story is humorous.

Read the story carefully and try to explain as precisely as possible why it is funny. Cite specific passages to back up your statements about it. Also, how does Twain use the story-within-a-story technique here? (I)

Mark Twain: *Tom Sawyer*

Tom Sawyer AS IT RELATES TO THE PRESENT DAY

How relevant does Tom Sawyer's boyhood seem to childhood in present-day America? What are the similarities and differences? Is identification with Tom Sawyer still possible?

Compare the picture of an American boyhood given in *Tom Sawyer* with what you know of America today in considering the above questions. (I)

Mark Twain: *Huckleberry Finn*
Tom Sawyer

A COMPARISON OF *Huckleberry Finn* AND *Tom Sawyer*

How does Huckleberry Finn differ from Tom Sawyer in spite of their basic similarity? How is it a more mature book with a broader scope?

Carefully read the two books. How do Huck and Tom differ in character? Does the relevance, meaning, and scope of *Huck Finn* exceed that of *Tom Sawyer*? How? Do you think there was a basic difference in the author's intentions in writing the two books? (II)

Walt Whitman: *Leaves of Grass*
(1855, 1856, 1860, 1867, 1871)

THE CHANGING TONE OF WALT WHITMAN

Show how the attitude of Whitman changes in the various editions of his Leaves of Grass.

Study and compare the several editions. What outlook seems to dominate in each? How does Whitman's poetic capability vary between editions? (III)

Walt Whitman: "Song of Myself"
Richard Chase: *Walt Whitman Reconsidered*
Roy Harvey Pearce: *The Continuity of American Poetry*

THE JOURNEY OF THE POET-HERO

Discuss Whitman's "Song of Myself" as a depiction of an heroic spirit which Whitman sees as inherent in the poet.

How is the poem a sort of spiritual journey? When does the man become a poet? In what way is the poet a creator? (II)

Walt Whitman: *Leaves of Grass*
John Dos Passos: *U.S.A.*

THE AMERICAN CATALOGUE: WHITMAN AND DOS PASSOS

Compare the use of the montage of images from the varied modes of American life in Whitman's Leaves of Grass *and Dos Passos'* U.S.A.

In what way are both Whitman and Dos Passos "democratic" artists? How does each use the context of juxtaposition for dramatic effect? Differentiate between the "celebration" of Whitman and the ironic sense of Dos Passos in their use of this technique? (II)

Henry James: *The Ambassadors*
Henry Adams: *The Education of Henry Adams*

The Ambassadors AND *The Education of Henry Adams*

Taking Adams' book as an intellectual history of the late nineteenth century, point out the parallels between James's novel and the thought of the times; the similarity of tone in the two books; the parallel between Strether and Adams.

With *The Education* in mind, consider Strether's career as the same sort of "education" as Adams' and point out the parallels in where they begin and end intellectually, the process by which they make their discoveries, and the effect on their personal consciousness. Try to delineate the philosophical trend of the era as a whole. (III)

Henry James: *Portrait of a Lady*

IDEALISM AND LOVE: JAMES' *Portrait of a Lady*

Analyze the Jamesian concept of love as delineated in this novel.

How does James regard Isabel's cousin's love for her? How does his love excel Isabel's relationship with her husband? What does her cousin try to teach her, and why does he go on loving her silently? (II)

Henry James: *Portrait of a Lady*

ISABEL ARCHER'S TRANSFORMATION

Discuss Portrait of a Lady.

How does Isabel Archer change in character in the course of the novel? What effect does each of the other main characters have on her? How do her various experiences with proposals and marriage affect her? (II)

England—20th Century

D. H. Lawrence: *The Man Who Died*

AN INVERSION OF THE CHRIST STORY

Do a study of Lawrence's The Man Who Died

How does Lawrence change or reverse the Christ story in this short novel? How does his book compare with the original account of Christ's life? What message does he convey by this radically altered Christ myth? (II)

D. H. Lawrence: *The Rainbow*

THE PROBLEM OF STRUCTURE IN *The Rainbow*

The Rainbow, by D. H. Lawrence, is fairly loose and episodic in its construction. How do the stories of the succeeding generations link up with one another? Is the book a success or a failure?

Examine the stories of each generation for common themes or other links of narrative. Try to decide whether you believe the book succeeds as a structured whole or whether it is merely episodic, and why. (II)

Dylan Thomas: "After the Funeral"

LINGUISTIC DISPLACEMENT IN "AFTER THE FUNERAL"

Discuss how Dylan Thomas achieves his effects in "After the Funeral."

Notice that Thomas makes extensive use of deliberately mixed metaphors and incongruous images, superimposing different trains of thought so as to produce an unexpected effect in the reader's mind. How do the usages work? What do they convey about the townspeople? About Thomas' feelings? (II)

Synge: Collected Works

RHYTHMIC USE OF COMMON SPEECH

Do an analysis of the language patterns in the work of Synge.

Determine what the various rhythms of the brogue are. How does Synge use them? Is there any use of melody? (III)

ENGLAND—20TH CENTURY

James Joyce: *A Portrait of the Artist As a Young Man*
Ulysses
Finnegan's Wake

THE MATURING OF JOYCE'S LITERATURE

Joyce once defined what he saw as the three progressively mature steps of artistry: the lyric, in which the artist sees within himself; the historic, in which he looks outside himself at other men; and the dramatic, in which he reunites his own spirit with these men. Apply this concept to the Daedalus trilogy.

How does the attitude of the protagonist in each successive volume parallel this development? How is this reflective of Joyce's own development as an artist? (III)

James Joyce: *The Dead*

THE PROSE STYLE OF JAMES JOYCE IN *The Dead*

Analyze Joyce's style in this story.

How does his style work—especially in the final pages? Indicate the poetic elements, if any. How does he use images? (II)

James Joyce: *Ulysses*
Homer: *Ulysses*

THE "SEARCH" MYTH

Analyze the "search" myth in Ulysses.

How is the "search" presented? What is its significance? Compare Joyce's use of "search" with that of Homer. (II)

E. M. Forster: *A Passage to India*
Plato: *The Republic*

TRANSFORMATION OF PLATONIC ALLEGORY

Discuss the use of the caves in A Passage to India.

Read Plato's comparison of man's life to the cave. Compare this allegory with the use of the caves in *A Passage to India*. How are they similar? How do they present different views of life? How does the allegory of the caves relate to the themes of the novel? (II)

E. M. Forster: *A Passage to India*
Howards End
Lionel Trilling: *E. M. Forster*

Howards End AND *A Passage to India*: FORSTER'S CHANGE IN WORLD VIEW

Explain the basic philosophical difference between Howards End *and* A Passage to India, *pointing out evidence of Forster's loss of faith in a unified world view. How does the move from unity to multiplicity reflect the intellectual events of the intervening years?*

Examine the symbolic and philosophical content of the two works and carefully explicate the basic difference between the two. Place this shift in the context of literature and history in the same period, particularly World War I. (II)

Harold Pinter: *The Dumb-Waiter*

THE SYMBOLISM OF *The Dumb-Waiter*

What symbolic implications can be seen in Pinter's The Dumb-Waiter? How do you derive these implications?

Consider the possible implications of all the action involving the dumb waiter. Can this be seen as a religious allegory of some sort? If so, what does it say about religion? What is the significance of the shooting at the end? (III)

G. B. Shaw: *Heartbreak House*

Heartbreak House AS THE TWENTIETH-CENTURY WORLD

Heartbreak House can be seen as the central play in Shaw's total statement. Derive from it Shaw's view of the condition of man in our times.

Consider the larger implications of the actions and speeches of the play. What does Shaw say about human relationships? About happiness? About intellectual pursuits? About money and business, etc.? Support your conclusions with specific quotes from the play. (III)

G. B. Shaw: *Man and Superman*

IRONY IN *Man and Superman*

Examine Shaw's ironic techniques in Man and Superman.

Show how both actions and speeches in the play are ironic. How does Shaw achieve this irony? Do any of the characters escape being deflated in the course of the play? Who emerges victorious, and why? Does the pervasive irony make the play seem totally skeptical, or not? (II)

T. S. Eliot: "The Waste Land"
John Donne: "The First Anniversary"

DECAYING WORLDS: DONNE AND ELIOT

Compare Donne's "The First Anniversary" and Eliot's "The Waste Land." In each there is a picture of a decaying world and some suggestion of a way out; explicate and compare the two.

What is the nature of the general decay pictured in each poem? What are the respective causes? How does each poet suggest a possible escape from the conditions of his time? What similarities are there across the gap of 300 years? (III)

Yeats: *At the Hawks Well*
Sotoba Komachi

YEATS AND THE ORIENTAL THEATRE

Investigate the devices of the Oriental theatre in the work of Yeats.

Examine the structure of Yeats' work closely. Compare and contrast the unconventional devices that he uses with the known conventions of the Oriental Theatre. (III)

E. M. Forster: *Howards End*
Lionel Trilling: *E. M. Forster*

THE SYMBOLIC STRUCTURE OF *Howards End*

How does the symbolism of Howards End *raise the specific story of the Schlegels and Wilcoxes to a general social picture of the times in which Forster wrote? How does the book become relevant to England as a whole and express Forster's social message?*

Consider the symbolic meaning of all the main characters in terms of the whole social structure of England at the time. How do they depict the past and project the future of English society? What is the significance of *Howards End* itself? Of Mrs. Wilcox? (II)

Sean O'Casey: *The Plough and the Stars*

STAGE DEVICES AND DRAMATIC CONTENT

What is the relationship between the dramatic devices employed in the play and the themes expressed by the play?

Note the use of various stage devices—for instance, the frequent intrusion of fire and the use made of doors and windows—and attempt to show how these devices bear on the message of the play and help to present it to us. (II)

Europe—20th Century

**Laurence Sterne: *Tristram Shandy*
Andre Gide: *The Counterfeiters*
*Journal of The Counterfeiters****

The Counterfeiters AND *Tristram Shandy*

Compare the narrative technique.

The fact that *Tristram* exists on more than one level and speaks to the reader directly gives us an ambiguous feeling; we wonder whether we are inside or outside the book. The use of multiple narrators and notebooks in *The Counterfeiters* leads to the same effect intensified, especially since the notebooks are for a novel entitled *The Counterfeiters*. Analyze and comment upon this effect in the two works. How do fiction and reality encroach upon each other in these books? (On this question, look at Gide's *Journal of The Counterfeiters*.) (III)

Marcel Proust: *Swann's Way*

STREAM OF CONSCIOUSNESS IN PROUST

Analyze the stream of consciousness devices and techniques which Proust employs, and evaluate their relevance to his themes. (II)

Albert Camus: *The Stranger*
Leo Tolstoy: *Anna Karenina*

TWO PHILOSOPHIES OF LIFE

A study of the philosophies of life of the characters Levin and Mersault.

Both Mersault and Levin come to terms with life and with themselves. Compare their resolutions. (II)

Camus: *Caligula*
Moliere: *Tartuffe*

A STUDY OF *Tartuffe* AND *Caligula*

Analyze the subject matter and techniques used by Camus and Moliere. (II)

Camus: *The Stranger*

WHAT POSSIBLE MOTIVE FOR MURDER?

Is the murder committed by Mersault meaningless?

What possible motives or exterior circumstances could have affected Mersault? What effect did his act have on him? What is the relation of this act to the rest of the book? (I)

Camus: *The Stranger*
The Myth of Sisyphus

REVERSAL OF A TRIAL

Society's trial of Mersault as Camus' trial of society.

Analyze Camus' attitude toward the individual and society as seen in *The Stranger*. (II)

Thomas Mann: *A Man and His Dog*
The Magic Mountain
Tonio Kroeger

LEITMOTIV IN MANN

Consider the settings and word patterns that occur in conjunction with various characters, moods, etc. Observe the ways in which these patterns recur. Why? What of the times when these patterns are absent? (II)

Thomas Mann: *The Magic Mountain*

THE RESOLUTION OF CONFLICTING PHILOSOPHIES IN *The Magic Mountain*

There are several separate philosophical systems represented in The Magic Mountain. *How does Mann resolve their conflict, and where does he stand among all of them?*

Viewing Hans Castorp as a sort of intellectual picaro, consider his reactions to all the ideas that surround him and how they affect him. How do the events of the plot relate to the ideas presented in the book? Consider especially the scene where Hans is alone in the snow-storm. Does Mann endorse any of the philosophies wholly? What does

Hans' final death (or disappearance) have to do with the ideas of the book? (III)

Strindberg: *The Dream Play*
Mann: *Tonio Kroeger*
Byron: *Don Juan*
Ibsen: *Peer Gynt*

"THE PETTY BOURGEOIS IS THE MAN WHO IS SATISFIED WITH HIMSELF"

Investigate what various authors would have thought about the above quote from Gorky.

Consider the attitude of Mann, Strindberg and Byron toward this quote. How would they interpret it? Would they approve? (II)

Thomas Mann: *Death in Venice*
Doctor Faustus

TWO VISIONS OF THE INTELLECTUAL LIFE IN MANN

Compare Death in Venice *and* Doctor Faustus.

In what ways are the two works similar? How do Aschenbach's and Leverkuhn's careers resemble each other? Why does a child figure so importantly in the life of each? How are these children similar? Could *Doctor Faustus* be viewed as an expansion of *Death in Venice* on a wider scale? What does Mann seem to be saying about the intellectual life in general? (III)

Franz Kafka: *Metamorphosis*
The Trial
The Castle

"AND SO THE CHOICE GOES BY FOREVER"
What is the role of choice in the world of Kafka?

Investigate the choices open to Kafka's characters. Are they real or chimerical? Consider how effective the results of these choices are. (III)

Mann: *Buddenbrooks*
Kafka: *The Castle*

CLASS WAR IN LITERATURE

A study of the relationship between Kafka and Mann.

Compare and contrast representative works from the two authors. It has been said that Mann relates to the bourgeois while Kafka's outlook was aristocratic. Is this apparent in these works? How did the differences in their philosophical outlook derive from their differences in social outlook? (II)

Thomas Mann: *Death In Venice*
Tonio Kroeger

THE LIFE OF THE ARTIST AS SEEN BY THOMAS MANN

What does Mann say about the artist's life in his two stories, Death in Venice *and* Tonio Kroeger?

Examine the two characters Aschenbach and Tonio Kroeger as examples of the artist's life. How does the artist relate to other people? Is art, in fact, the essence of life? Is art a purely intellectual function or not? (II)

Mann: *Felix Krull*

FELIX KRULL AS THE PICARO

A study of Mann's character, Felix Krull.

Consider Krull's approach to life. Is this picaresque? Are the reactions of the other characters appropriate to Krull as a picaro? (II)

Franz Kafka: *Before the Law*
The Penal Colony

BEFORE THE LAW: THE KAFKAESQUE PREDICAMENT

Examine and discuss the "Law" in Kafka.

What kind of "Law" is it? Is it just? Who are the people who operate the "Law"? Who are those who "benefit" from it? (I)

Franz Kafka: *The Penal Colony*
Country Doctor
And Other Selections

THE PHENOMENOLOGY OF FRANZ KAFKA

Examine Kafka's works in terms of phenomenological concepts.

What is phenomenology? How does it apply to Kafka? Is phenomenology the *end* for Kafka, or does he see it as an alternative? (II)

Camus: *Caligula*

CAMUS ON *Caligula*

"I look in vain for a philosophy in these four acts. Or, if it exists, it stands on the level of this assertion by the hero: 'Men die; and they are not happy.' . . . No, my ambition lay elsewhere. For the dramatist, the study of the impossible is just as valid a subject for study as avarice or adultery. Showing it in all its frenzy, illustrating the havoc

it wreaks, bringing out its failure—such was my intention. And the work must be judged thereon."

Does the playwright succeed in his intention, and does his comment help understanding? (III)

20th Century Drama

Bertolt Brecht: *Baal*

BRECHT ON *Baal*

"I hope in Baal ... I've avoided one common artistic blooper, that of trying to carry people away. Instinctively, I've kept my distance and ensured that the realization of my poetical and philosophical effects remains within bounds. The spectator's 'splendid isolation' is left intact."

Does the playwright succeed in his intention? Does his comment help understanding? (III)

Gay: *The Beggar's Opera*
Brecht: *Die Dreigroschenoper*

The Beggar's AND *Three Penny Opera*

How has Brecht adapted the story and why?

Compare and contrast the two texts. (II)

Brecht: *The Good Woman of Sechzuan*
Mother Courage
The Caucasian Chalk Circle

EPIC THEATRE

What does Brecht mean by Epic Theatre?

Consider those factors in the work of Brecht which set Brecht off from the other dramatists.
(II)

Brecht: *The Good Woman of Sechzuan*
           Baal

THE EXPRESSIONISTIC BRECHT

Prepare a study of the characteristics of Brecht's Expressionistic work.

Compare and contrast *Baal* with a later work. Why is *Baal* expressionistic? (II)

Brecht: *Mother Courage*
           Mahagonny
           The Resistible Rise of Arturo Ui
Jean Genet: *The Maids*
               The Balcony

THE THEATRICAL ILLUSION IN BRECHT AND GENET

Discuss how these two playwrights treat the theatrical medium in a radically new way.

"In modern drama, playwrights have ceased to struggle against the artificiality of theatre or to attempt a convincing reality on stage; instead they emphasize the illusory nature of theatre and use its artificialities for new ends." Discuss, with quotes from the authors to support your statements. (III)

John Webster: *The White Devil*
Samuel Beckett: *Endgame*

The White Devil AND *Endgame*

Compare and contrast the behavior of the plays' characters.

Both plays deal with worlds without morals. How do the characters have any meaning in these worlds? (III)

Eugene Ionesco: *Amedee*

IONESCO ON *Amedee*

"Amedee, *whose action takes place in the apartment of a petty bourgeois family, is a realistic play into which I introduced fantastic elements which served both to destroy the realism and to underline it.*"

Does the playwright succeed in his intention, and does his comment help understanding? (II)

Samuel Beckett: *Endgame*
Harold Pinter: *The Dumb-Waiter*

PINTER AND BECKETT

Pinter and Beckett are both generally thought of as absurd dramatists. What differences, rather than similarities, exist between them?

Compare *The Dumb-Waiter* to *Endgame* in dramatic technique, use of stage devices, use of symbolism, and possible implications. Pay attention to the problem of communication among the characters in each. (II)

Feydeau: *Madame's Late Lamented Mother*
Ionescu: *Amedee*
Albee: *The Sandbox*

PATTERNS OF INFLUENCE IN FEYDEAU, IONESCO AND ALBEE

Trace the line of descent in these three modern dramatists.

Modern dramatists are frequently so aware of their predecessors that the line of descent is often easy to follow. (II)

Albee: *The Sandbox*
Beckett: *Waiting for Godot*
Ionescu: *Amedee*
  Rhinoceros
Pinter: *The Caretakers*
  Adamov
  Professor Taranne

THE CHARACTERISTICS OF THE THEATRE OF THE ABSURD: HUMOR

Analyze how the use of humor by the Absurdist authors characterizes their work. Is the use of humor intended merely for comic effect? Humor may often be employed as a superficially entertaining medium while in essence it is penetrating and exposing harsh realities. How does the Theatre of the Absurd incorporate both of these factors? What complex effect on the reader or audience is produced during the play? After?

Many characters of the Theatre of the Absurd are manifestations of universal internal fears and frustrations, while on stage they simply appear eccentric. What reactions do such characters elicit from the audience? (II)

Strindberg: *The Dream Play*
Wedekind: *Spring's Awakening*
Brecht: *Baal*

PATTERNS OF INFLUENCE IN STRINDBERG, WEDEKIND, BRECHT

Trace the line of descent in these three modern dramatists.

Modern dramatists are frequently so aware of their predecessors that the line of descent is often easy to follow. (II)

Beckett: *Molloy*
Malone Dies
The Unnamable
Kerouac: *On the Road*
The Dharma Bums
The Railroad Earth

The Absurdist and Beat Novels

Analyze the similarities and differences between Absurd and Beat novels.

Compare typical texts, wtih special reference to theme, style, etc. (III)

Beckett: *Waiting for Godot*

Becket on Waiting for Godot

"Habit is the ballast that chains the dog to his vomit. Breathing is habit. Life is habit. Or rather life is a succession of habits, since the individual is a succession of individuals ... Habit then is the generic term for the countless treaties concluded between the countless subjects that constitute the countless individuals and their countless correlative objects. The periods of transition that separate consecutive adaptations ... represent the perilous zones in the life of the individual, dangerout, precarious, painful, mysterious and fertile, when for a moment the boredom of living is replaced by the suffering of being."

Does the playwright succeed in his intention, and does his comment help toward an understanding of the play? (III)

Camus: *Caligula*
Beckett: *Waiting for Godot*
Pinter: *The Caretaker*

PATTERNS OF INFLUENCE IN CAMUS, BECKETT, PINTER

Trace the line of descent in these three modern dramatists.

Modern dramatists are frequently so aware of their predecessors, that the line of descent is often easy to follow. (III)

Jean Genet: *The Balcony*

ILLUSION AND REALITY IN *The Balcony*

Discuss the play's statement on the theme of illusion and reality, and the use of illusion in the play to bear on that theme.

The play basically concerns a house of prostitution which might be thought of as a house of illusion, and a rebellion of reality against illusion. What, to Genet, is real? Is anything wholly illusory or wholly real, or are the two inextricably mingled? How does the use of stage devices, costumes, and other illusory stage effects relate to the theme of the play? (III)

Beckett: *Waiting for Godot*
Ionesco: *The Bald Soprano*
Victims of Duty
Ferlinghetti: *Unfair Arguments with Existence*
Routines

ABSURDIST AND BEAT DRAMA

Compare the characteristic dramas of the two schools, Beat and Absurd.

Do a point-by-point comparison of theme, style, etc. of major dramatic works of the two schools.
(II)

Ionescu: *Amedee*
The Chairs
The New Tenant

THE PROLIFERATION OF THINGS

Investigate the "proliferation of things" in the work of Ionesco.

Is the proliferation of things a thematic or a stylistic device? What does Ionesco achieve with it? What is the relationship of this theme to his philosophy? (II)

America—20th Century

Theodore Dreiser: *Sister Carrie*
An American Tragedy

NATURALISM IN AMERICA

A Study of American mores and values.

How does Dreiser depict the destructive, corrosive quality of industrial American society? What are the forces that contribute to the downfall of the main characters in the two novels? (II)

John Steinbeck: *Grapes of Wrath*

Grapes of Wrath: A PHILOSOPHICAL AND SOCIOLOGICAL APPROACH

Does Steinbeck reveal a fatalistic philosophy in Grapes of Wrath? *(Consider the evolution of some of the main characters and their changing reactions to an impoverished existence.)*

Is Steinbeck attempting merely social protest or does he indirectly offer various suggestions for social reform? Use various plot incidents and characters for support. (II)

William Faulkner: *The Sound and the Fury*
Edmond L. Volpe: *A Reader's Guide to William Faulkner*

AN ANALYSIS OF THE FIRST SECTION OF *The Sound and the Fury*

The first section of The Sound and the Fury, *narrated by the idiot Benjy, prepares us for the rest of the book if we can penetrate the confusion of his narrative style. How does Benjy's mind work in this narration; what main events does he touch on; how does he feel about them; and how does this prepare the reader for what follows?*

Study the section carefully, attempting to place the time shifts in the narrative and to describe the actual events and their importance to Benjy and the book as a whole. (II)

Edmond L. Volpe: *A Reader's Guide to William Faulkner*

MEN AND WOMEN IN FAULKNER

How do the men and women in Faulkner differ psychologically, especially in their approach to life, and how does this help in defining the tragic heroism of the men?

Examine Eula Varner in *The Hamlet*, Lena Grove of *Light in August* or Addie Bundren in *As I Lay Dying*, with regard to the above question. Then compare any of these women with Quentin Compson of *The Sound and the Fury* or Bayard Sartoris of *Sartoris* and attempt to answer the question fully. (II)

William Faulkner: *Absalom, Absalom!*

Absalom, Absalom!: NOVEL OR POLEMIC?

Absalom, Absalom! differs greatly from most novels in presenting very little direct action and consisting almost solely of narration of past events by the characters. Should the book in fact be termed a novel, or should it be viewed as a vehicle for Faulkner's personal statement about the South?

Examine and point out the ways in which *Absalom, Absalom!* differs from normal novelistic techniques and the consequent effects on the reader. Try to present your own reaction as precisely as possible and your arguments for or against classifying it as a novel. (II)

William Faulkner: *Sartoris*

FUTILITY AND HEROISM IN *Sartoris*

Many members of the Sartoris clan, from the original Sartoris to the last one, lead heroic lives and yet die for essentially pointless reasons. How does the futility of their actions relate to their heroism? Is it not an essential part of that heroism, and why?

Consider the lives of Bayard Sartoris, I and the brothers Bayard and John and attempt to assess

why the pointlessness of their deaths is an inherent part of their tragic heroism. Why is Bayard, I's death in pursuit of a can of anchovies more heroic than otherwise? What does this say about these men? About tragic action? About heroic action?
(I)

William Faulkner: *Light in August*

JOE CHRISTMAS AS A CHRIST-FIGURE

A study of possible Christ symbolism in the central character of Light in August.

Much evidence in the book points toward an identification of Joe Christmas with Christ. Discuss this evidence. How does the Christ reference relate to the themes of the book? (II)

William Faulkner: *Go Down, Moses*

THE RELATION OF WHITE TO NEGRO IN *Go Down, Moses*

What is the pattern of relations between the white McCaslins and their illegitimate Negro relatives? How are attitudes different in successive generations of McCaslins and how do they deal with their guilt about their treatment of the Negro?

Construct the genealogy of the McCaslins, including the Negro branch. Examine how the succeeding plantation owners, down to Roth Edmonds, deal with the Negro, giving special attention to the two pivotal figures of Lucas Beauchamp and Ike McCaslin. How does the McCaslin family lose its vitality, and how does this relate to their attitude toward the land and the Negro? (II)

Thomas Wolfe: *Look Homeward, Angel*

"A Stone, A Leaf, An Unfound Door"

A discussion of recurrent images in Look Homeward, Angel.

What are the images that occur throughout the book? How do they relate to Wolfe's themes? Is their continual use effective or does it become tiresome? Why? How is the use of recurrent images an integral part of Wolfe's style? (II)

Thomas Wolfe: *Of Time and the River*
Look Homeward, Angel
You Can't Go Home Again
The Web and the Rock

The Search for the Father in Thomas Wolfe

Analyze the quest of the protagonist in the four major novels of Wolfe in terms of a search for the strength and the spirit of a father.

How does the father represent for both Eugene Gant and Monk Webber a spirit free from the oppression of human existence? Is the protagonist ever able to satisfy or reconcile this search? (II)

Robert Lowell: "Skunk Hour"
E. E. Cummings "Pity This Busy Monster, Mankind"

Lowell and Cummings

Both poems may be taken as fairly general statements, but they differ almost completely in tone, technique, and meaning. Comment upon the differences between these two important modern poets.
(II)

Evelyn Waugh: *Decline and Fall*

WAUGH AS A MORALIST

Consider Decline and Fall *and determine Waugh's judgment of his characters.*

What is the purpose of Waugh's satiric technique? Is his touch light, or damning? (I)

Nathanael West: *The Day of the Locust*

WEST'S VIEW OF THE WORLD IN *The Day of the Locust*

A discussion of how West portrays the modern world in this work.

Is West's book only about Hollywood, or does it reflect on all of America (or mankind in general)? How does West portray American society? What are the mores and motivations of the people in the book? How do you react to them? (Optionally, consider how this compares to Eliot's world-picture in *The Waste Land*, Lawrence's in *St. Mawr*, or Fitzgerald's in *The Great Gatsby*.) (II)

Nathanael West: *Miss Lonelyhearts*

MISS LONELYHEARTS AS A CHRIST-FIGURE

Assess the possibility that Miss Lonelyhearts may be intended as a Christ-figure.

Note the frequent mention of Christ and things connected with Christ (often sarcastically by Shrike) and the similarities between some of Miss Lonelyhearts' actions and those of Christ. Do you see the similarity as being intended to function symbolically? Does it connect to the themes of the story? Or is it only ironical? Cite specific evidence for your point of view. (II)

E. E. Cummings: *The Enormous Room*
Henry Fielding: *Tom Jones*
Thomas Nashe: *The Unfortunate Traveler*
or other Picaresque Novels

The Enormous Room AS AN INTERIOR-PICARESQUE NOVEL

Compare The Enormous Room *to a picaresque novel, showing the similarities in structure and technique and the difference in total effect.*

Although it does not involve a large amount of traveling, *The Enormous Room* bears a strong resemblance in structure and technique to traditional picaresque novels such as Nashe's *The Unfortunate Traveler* or Fielding's *Tom Jones*. Pick such a novel and explain the similarities as well as the different total result. (III)

The Poetry of Frost and Stevens

THE RELATION OF POETRY TO EXPERIENCE: FROST AND WALLACE STEVENS

Compare and contrast, with a poem of each author, the effect of experience on poetry, its language and form.

Examine the theme in terms of metaphor and poetic form. (III)

The Poetry of Stevens and Whitman

THE RELATION OF POETRY TO EXPERIENCE:
   STEVENS AND WHITMAN

Compare and contrast, with a poem of each author, the effect of experience on poetry, its language and form.

Examine theme in terms of metaphor and poetic form. (III)

Ernest Hemingway: *The Sun Also Rises*
   A Farewell to Arms
   The Old Man and the Sea
   Death in the Afternoon

HEMINGWAY'S HEROES

Compare and contrast various heroes. What do they have in common? How does Hemingway treat them?

What is Hemingway's concept of the hero? (II)

Ernest Hemingway: *The Short Happy Life*
      of Francis Macomber
D. H. Lawrence: *The Ladybird*
   The Fox

HEMINGWAY AND LAWRENCE

Compare The Short Happy Life of Francis Macomber *and* The Ladybird.

In what ways are these stories similar in theme? Do Lawrence and Hemingway offer any ideas in common? Are the conflicts in the stories at all similar? In the Hemingway story, where does the "Short Happy Life" begin? (II)

F. Scott Fitzgerald: *The Great Gatsby*
Tender Is the Night

SYMBIOTIC NATURE OF LOVE IN FITZGERALD

Show how Fitzgerald sees love as a process in which one partner lives from the strength of the other.

Study the love of Gatsby and Daisy and of Dick and Nicolle Diver. What is the progressive effect of this love and the fate of the stronger partner? Does the author offer any possibiilty of a non-destructive love? (II)

F. Scott Fitzgerald: *The Great Gatsby*
Tender Is the Night

THE ONCE-BURNING FLAME: SCOTT FITZGERALD ON AMERICAN LIFE

Fitzgerald once said that there are no "second acts" in the characters of America. Apply this concept to the stories of Dick Diver and Jay Gatsby.

Show how the lives of the two men climaxed in such a way that, given their respective characters, there was no other possible result. (II)

J. D. Salinger: *The Laughing Man*

A STORY WITHIN A STORY

Assess the relationship between Salinger's story, The Laughing Man, *as a whole, and the story of the Laughing Man told by the Chief within it.*

How does the tale of the Laughing Man, told by the Chief, bear on the story as a whole? How does it help the effect of the story? Would it be possible to have the same story without the tale of the Laughing Man? (I)

J. D. Salinger: *The Catcher in the Rye*

HOW CONTEMPORARY IS HOLDEN CAULFIELD?

Discussion of problems concerning today's youth and those faced by Holden Caulfield.

Is there a universal nature to the character of Holden Caulfield? Examine his relationship to his family, his school, his city, etc. Show any parallels with adolescents of today. (II)

Kerouac: *The Dharma Bums*
On the Road
Wolfe: *Look Homeward, Angel*
Of Time and the River

WOLFE'S INFLUENCE ON KEROUAC

Explore Wolfe's relationship to Kerouac.

Compare and contrast typical works by the two authors. What elements of Wolfe's form, style, etc. can be found in Kerouac? (II)

Sherwood Anderson: *Winesburg, Ohio*
Malcolm Cowley: Introduction to the Compass Edition of *Winesburg, Ohio*

AN EXPLICATION OF *Winesburg, Ohio*

An analysis of the central themes of Winesburg, Ohio *and how they show up in the stories.*

Consider "The Book of the Grotesque" and "Tandy" as they embody the central themes of the whole book; explicate these themes, and show how they bear on the other stories. What points does the book make as a whole? How is its narrative technique related to its content? (I)

Robert Penn Warren: *All the King's Men*

CASS MASTERN AND JACK BURDEN

What is the relationship between the story of Cass Mastern and that of Jack Burden in Warren's All the King's Men?

Explore the similarities between the Cass Mastern story and the entire book in structure and meaning. Could the book as a whole have grown out of the Cass Mastern story? (II)

William Carlos Williams:
"The Red Wheelbarrow" in *How Does a Poem Mean?* by John Ciardi

MEANING BEHIND THE POEM: "THE RED WHEELBARROW"

William Carlos Williams' poem, "The Red Wheelbarrow" consists of only sixteen works; yet it suggests many ideas and meanings. What does it suggest to you, and why?

Try to explain everything that the poem suggests to you as you read it. Why does it have more meaning than its length would suggest? For instance, what do you make of "so much" in the first line? Are there any metaphors in the poem? Could the whole poem be considered a metaphor?
(I)

Gregory Corso: *Gasoline and Other Poems*

"WHAT WAS GARCIA LORCA DOING BY THE WATERMELONS?"

An analysis of the meaning of the above line.

Determine the function of the line in the body of the poem as a whole. Investigate how it supports the development of the theme and how it fits in with the stylistic patterns. (III)

Allen Ginsburg: *Howl*
Lawrence Ferlinghetti: *A Coney Island of the Mind*

CATALOGING IN GINSBURG AND FERLINGHETTI

What do the poets intend to convey with the use of cataloging? How does this relate to their other image patterns? (II)

Ferlinghetti: "I Am Waiting"

A study of form in Ferlinghetti's poem.

Examine the text. What form does it exhibit? How does the form contribute to the over-all effect of the poem? (II)

The Poetry of Frost and Eliot

EVALUATION OF REALITY: FROST AND ELIOT

Compare and contrast, with a poem of each author, their views of reality.

Examine all aspects of their treatments of the theme, including uses of language and poetic form. (III)

AMERICA—20TH CENTURY

Arthur Miller: *The Crucible*

The Crucible AS SOCIAL CRITICISM

How does The Crucible *relate to the times in which it was written and provide a criticism of them?*

Compare the events of *The Crucible* to the investigations of the McCarthy era. What parallels can be drawn? What statement about that era can be derived from Miller's play? (II)

O'Neill: *The Iceman Cometh*
Miller: *Death of a Salesman*

HICKY AND BIFF LOMAN

Compare and contrast these characters.

How is each characterized? How do they affect the dramatic action? (II)

Edward Albee: *The Sandbox*

SOCIAL SATIRE IN *The Sandbox*

Examine Albee's use of satire.

What is satirical in this work? Is the satire a major factor or is it incidental? Try to separate the significant from the merely relevant. (II)

Wilder: *The Happy Journey from Trenton to Camden*
O'Neill: *Mourning Becomes Electra*
The Emperor Jones
Long Day's Journey into Night
Albee: *The Sandbox*

Originality in the American Theatre

Critics of the American Theatre frequently accuse it of provincialism and imitation, claiming it has no originalty.

Make a case for or against the creativity of American dramatists, taking as examples Wilder, O'Neill and Albee, and referring when necessary to innovations in European theatre that influenced them. (III)

Ralph Ellison: *The Invisible Man*
Richard Wright: *Native Son*

Two Views of the Black Experience in America

Compare the heroes of both novels.

Discuss how each confronts the complexities of black life in America; how he deals with the white world, and how he strives for confirmation of his manhood. (I)

Norman Mailer: *The Armies of the Night*
Miami and the Siege of Chicago

The Novelist as Historian

Discuss Mailer's style of reportage.

Does Mailer's involvement throughout these works serve to vitalize or weaken the telling of the events? Does his personality distract from or add to an understanding of his subject? Do you think a greater objectivity is more appropriate for the historian? (I)

Get High-Powered Marks in Your English Courses
ARCO LITERARY CRITIQUES

A new approach to the study of the great writers of English literature. Arco Literary Critiques guide you through the maze of critical material, clearly analyzing the essentials of each work and presenting them in such a way as to provide concise, useful material for classroom discussion, term papers, book reports and tests. Each book is illustrated and contains 128 to 160 pages.

$1.95 each

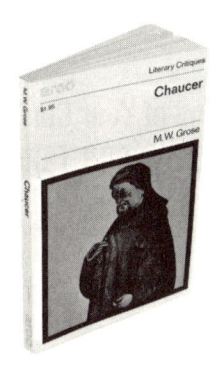

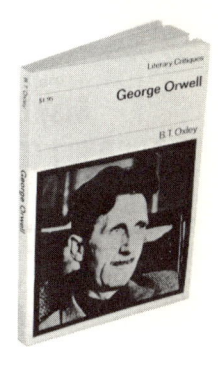

MATTHEW ARNOLD
JANE AUSTEN
BLAKE
CHARLOTTE AND EMILY BRONTË
ROBERT BROWNING
BYRON
CHAUCER
CONRAD
T. S. ELIOT
FIELDING
E. M. FORSTER
THOMAS HARDY
KEATS
D. H. LAWRENCE
MILTON
GEORGE ORWELL
SCOTT
SHAKESPEARE
GEORGE BERNARD SHAW
SWIFT
TENNYSON
THACKERAY
W. B. YEATS

All books are available at your bookseller or directly from ARCO PUBLISHING COMPANY INC., 219 Park Avenue South, New York, N.Y. 10003. Send price of books plus 25¢ for postage and handling. Sorry, no C.O.D.

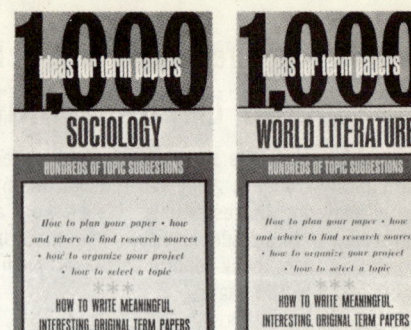

Stay On Top of Your Classwork with
ARCO'S 1,000 IDEAS FOR TERM PAPER SERIES

Concise yet thorough guides to the planning and preparation of term papers for high school and college students—how to plan the paper, how and where to find research sources, how to organize the project, how to select a topic. $1.95 each, except where noted.

1,000 IDEAS FOR TERM PAPERS IN:

AMERICAN HISTORY
From pre-revolutionary times to the post-World War II period.

ECONOMICS
From macroeconomic theory to the literature of Smith, Marx, Keynes.

ENGLISH
From Chaucer to modern realism. **1.45**

SOCIAL SCIENCE
Topics on psychology, anthropology, sociology and political science.

SOCIOLOGY
Communications, war, urbanization, family, criminology, research design, analysis of data.

WORLD LITERATURE
From Beowulf to the twentieth century.

All books are available at your bookseller or directly from ARC BOOKS INC., 219 Park Avenue South, New York, N.Y. 10003. Send price of books plus 25¢ postage and handling. Sorry no C.O.D.